How Creativity is Changing China

Li Wuwei

Edited by Michael Keane
Translated by Hui Li and Marina Guo

BLOOMSBURY ACADEMIC

First published in 2011 by

Bloomsbury Academic
an imprint of Bloomsbury Publishing Plc
36 Soho Square, London W1D 3QY, UK
and
175 Fifth Avenue, New York, NY 10010, USA

CIP records for this book are available from the British Library and the Library of Congress

ISBN 978-1-84966-619-0 (hardback)
ISBN 978-1-84966-616-9 (paperback)
ISBN 978-1-84966-658-9 (ebook)

This book is produced using paper that is made from wood grown in managed, sustainable
forests. It is natural, renewable and recyclable. The logging and manufacturing processes conform
to the environmental regulations of the country of origin.

Printed and bound in Great Britain by the MPG Books Group, Bodmin, Cornwall

Cover designer: Mark Penfound
Cover image: Stock.XCHNG©bhavitnaik

www.bloomsburyacademic.com

How Creativity is Changing China

Contents

List of Illustrations

List of Tables

Editor's Introduction

Michael Keane

It is a very rare event when a book by a senior Chinese policy advisor gets published in English. More often the accepted format is biography or auto-biography, generally published once the person has retired.

This book was first published by Xinhua Press in Chinese in a longer version in 2009. Initially it was directed at the Chinese reader, more specifically the Chinese cultural academic, and for this reason some of the material is not repeated in this abridged version. Nevertheless, it is important to point out that the author represents four speaking positions, and the messages that emerge from this work need to be contextualized accordingly.

First, Li Wuwei is a researcher with a background in industrial economics, econometrics and economic management. In China, where reform is the operative principle of economic, social and cultural development, economists have a leading role in policy advocacy. Industrial economics in China largely concerns what a traditional Chinese Marxist scholar might call the 'productive forces', namely the combination of natural resources, government policy, competitive markets, infrastructure, human capital, and business strategy. Increasingly in China we notice these factors aggregated as inputs of 'capital': intellectual capital, structural capital, technological capital, human capital, cultural capital etc. Essentially, this approach infers that these 'capitals' can be 'upgraded', which may take place through investment or through the self-organizing activities of the market itself. In the book we thus find the term 'upgrading' used frequently.

Second, Li is a senior policy advisor. He is a Vice-Chairperson of the National Committee of the Chinese People's Political Consultative Conference (CPPCC) and a Vice-Chairperson of the Central Committee of the Chinese Kuomintang Revolutionary Committee. The CPPCC dates back to pre-Liberation times when both the Chinese Communist Party (CCP) and the Kuomintang (Guomindang) agreed to form an alliance in the post-war period, that is after the Japanese imperialists had been defeated. The first 'conference' was held in Chongqing in 1946. When the Kuomintang moved to Taiwan in 1949 under the leadership of Chiang Kai-Chek (Jiang Jieshi) following the establishment of the PRC, the title Chinese People's Political Consultative Conference was conferred. In many respects this Conference operates as an advisory group for legislators and includes 'minor democratic parties'.

The Chinese Kuomintang Revolutionary Committee is the most influential of the eight sanctioned minor political parties in China. One of its important roles is to provide policy advocacy as a participating party in the framework of a multi-party cooperation system under CCP's leadership. The central government often attaches great importance to their proposals. Initially founded with a more left-wing policy agenda than its exiled parent, it maintains considerable assets throughout China. In effect, Li's position representing the Kuomintang in both these groups allows him to input directly into national policy in a unique way and offers the chance to express perspectives that are perhaps less orthodox while still aligned with the general development project of the nation-state. In addition to these official roles, Li is also Director of the Shanghai Creative Industries Association, which was formed in 2004. This group operates out of Shanghai and has been responsible for the rapid dissemination of local policies that have facilitated Shanghai's emergence as arguably the creative industries capital of China.

Thirdly, Li is a researcher, an educator, and a Professor at the Shanghai Academy of Social Sciences where he was the former Director of the Industrial Economics Institute, and more recently the Director of the Research Centre for Creative Industries. The book therefore functions as a textbook for researchers in the centre and presents the latest thinking on how China is applying this international development concept in theory and in practice.

Finally, Li Wuwei is an independent thinker: a person who by virtue of the above three positions is able to offer a somewhat different perspective on China's reforms than what the non-Chinese reader might expect from central officials. Li was born in Dongyang city in Zhejiang Province in 1942. While he is obviously associated with developments in the Shanghai municipality, Li constantly travels around China introducing his ideas. By virtue of his background in economics and his political seniority he is regarded nationally as the leading spokesperson on the cultural and creative industries in China; he invariably opens major economic development conferences and 'international cultural and creative industries expos' which have become a feature of the Chinese cultural scene in the past few years.

The Power of an Idea

How Creativity is Changing China is a book about the diffusion of an idea into the People's Republic of China. The idea is that creativity is essential for the renewal of Chinese society. While it might seem strange to suggest that China lacks creativity – for instance, think of the splendour of Song landscape art, Tang poetry, its exquisite bronzes, a rich and colourful language – there is a widespread view within China that the nation's well of creativity has run low and needs ways to refresh itself. But what does the word creativity now mean in China? Is it something that can be stimulated from the top or is it more about wider social transformation? Indeed, Li's view is that China is moving towards a creative society, which is a more specific indicator of cultural progress than the slogan 'harmonious society', which is used to refer to all facets of people's lives.

The following section fills in background necessary to understand what has been a major turning point in the administration of cultural policy in China. Something quite remarkable is taking place. It seems that China is overflowing with artists, animators, designers, and writers. Ideas like creativity and innovation appear constantly in the press and in Chinese television reports. The internet, which now has over 400 million users, is generating more and more users *and uses*.[1] How has this come about? Does this really portend a creative society?

The Chinese creative society may be a long way off – 2020 in Li's reckoning – but its roots go back to the 1990s, a decade when the terms 'cultural market' and 'cultural industries' became accepted ways of describing the secularization of Chinese culture. By secularization I refer to the fact that Chinese culture, even representational art, from the 1940s until the 1990s was effectively aligned to ideology. In the past scholars used the terms 'official mainstream culture' and 'engineers of the soul' to describe the supervision of cultural workers and their role in propaganda work.

---

[1] From 2008 to 2010 China jumped twenty places in the World Economic Forum's Global Networked Readiness Rankings, from 57 to 37. See http://www.weforum.org/pdf/GITR10/TheNetworkedReadinessIndexRankings.pdf [accessed 8 March 2011]. For a discussion of alternative uses of the internet see Jack Qiu, *Working Class Network Society: Communication Technology and the Information Have-Less in Urban China* (Cambridge: MIT Press, 2009).

Cultural forms were mechanisms of social reform. The mass media assumed a central 'guiding' role. The kind of subject sanctioned by cultural propaganda in the Maoist era was a self-sacrificing, altruistic collective subject. People were called to undergo conversion to the cause of revolution, following which they were trained to be socialist citizens. The Chinese subject was moulded through cultural propaganda disseminated in the educational system, in study sessions, and through the mass media.

Dramatic changes took place in Chinese society during the 1980s and 1990s. Many of these changes were directly attributed to the Chinese Communist Party's economic reforms presided over by Deng Xiaoping. These reforms were wide-ranging, not only in the sense of re-aligning material interests, but also in seeking to change people's conduct, to make people more productive and less dependent on the state. Upon assuming leadership in 1978, Deng distanced his government from the chaos of the Cultural Revolution (1966–1976) and sought to redefine people's roles as Chinese subjects. Deng's endorsement of wealth creation stands out as perhaps the most definitive break with the egalitarian social policies of the Mao Zedong era. Deng's much-quoted dictum 'to get rich is glorious' quickly led to aspirations of success and prosperity. At the same time Deng spoke of the idea of a *xiaokang* society; that is, a 'moderately prosperous society', one in which all people are well off in a way similar to developed countries in the West.

The role that cultural representations played in the remaking of the Chinese social consciousness during the People's Revolution cannot be underestimated. However, the Chinese propensity for wealth creation is a longer story than this short interval within a long history. It is almost as if the denial of the market under revolutionary socialism was an aberration. At the end of the Cultural Revolution the mood had changed from revolution to reform, from the iron rice bowl system of social welfare to a market economy, albeit one in which the government still played a guiding role. The cultural market took shape more gradually. The US scholar Richard Kraus wrote, 'State-sponsored culture, when no longer a monopoly, must contend for audiences, rather than take them for granted, and runs the risk of becoming irrelevant',[2] an idea encapsulated in Zha Jianying's *China Pop*, the first book length account in English of China's new

[2] Richard Kraus, *The Party and the Arty in China: the New Politics of Culture* (Lanham, Boulder: Rowman and Littlefield, 2004, p. 64).

secular culture.[3] Cultural production expanded as people's livelihood moved away from complete reliance on the state. Cultural producers were forced to survive with reduced state funding.

Following the Third Plenum of the 11th Central Committee of the CCP in 1978, China's cultural sphere began to change. In the 1980s China cautiously opened its doors to the outside world. New terms seeped into the Chinese lexicon competing with the ever-present political slogans. The Western world, and in particular the US entertainment industries began to make plans to enter China, some moguls thinking that it would be a simple matter of offering a choice of television programs and magazines.[4] The early 1980s witnessed a first stage of media liberalization but it would be a long time before Western media could make inroads. The principal organs of publicity – television, press and radio – were alerted to the task of seeking alternative financing arrangements.

A noteworthy landmark in cultural production was the rehabilitation of advertising. During the previous three decades of socialism, the creative potential of China's cultural workers had been subsumed in the promoting of Party doctrines. Propaganda was in effect state advertising. Under a system in which cultural goods were produced according to quotas and distributed according to plan, product advertising was redundant and even considered wasteful. On January 28 1979, China's first television advertisement appeared promoting a herbal wine on Shanghai television. A month later viewers witnessed the first foreign advertisement, a promotion for the Westinghouse Corporation.

---

[3] Jianying Zha, *China Pop: How Soap Operas, Tabloids, and Bestsellers Are Transforming a Culture* (New York: The New Press, 1995). A number of excellent books, and many articles, have been written since then. These include Orville Schell and Jim Jorgensen, *Mandate of Heaven: A New Generation of Entrepreneurs, Dissidents, Bohemians and Technocrats Lays Claim to China's Future* (New York: Simon & Schuster, 1995); Shuyu Kong, *Consuming Literature: Best Sellers and the Commercialization of Literary Production in Contemporary China* (Stanford CA: Stanford University Press, 2005); Richard C. Kraus, *The Party and the Arty in China: the New Politics of Culture* (Lanham, Boulder: Rowman and Littlefield, 2004); Jing Wang, *Brand New China: Advertising, Media and Commercial Culture* (Cambridge, Mass.: Harvard University Press, 2008): Liu Kang, *Globalization and Cultural Trends in China* (Honolulu: University of Hawaii Press, 2004); Claire Huot, *China's New Cultural Scene: A Handbook of Changes* (Durham: Duke University Press, 2000). Special journal issues on China's creative industries include the *International Journal of Cultural Studies* 9 (3), 2006; *The Chinese Journal of Communication* 1 (2), 2009; and the *Creative Industries Journal* 1 (3), 2010.

[4] For instance see the account of Rupert Murdoch's China ambitions in Bruce Dover, *Rupert's Adventures in China: How Murdoch Lost a Fortune and Found a Wife* (Penguin Viking, London, 2007).

In November 1979, the CCP Central Committee had formally ratified advertising in the mass media.

While advertising heralded the rising power of the audience, changes in the media were incremental and cautious, and more about decentralising financial responsibility than changing the pedagogical role of the media; it was not until the early 1990s, following Deng Xiaoping's 1992 'southern tour' to the new territories of Shenzhen that the investment model for cultural production began to change.

The 1990s witnessed a release of productive capacity in China. The market became the *de facto* logic of reform. With the expansion of private enterprise, much of it financed by international investment, China moved inexorably towards integration into the global economy. As international business waited in anticipation for protectionist barriers to fall, the problem of stimulating productive forces continued to confront Chinese reformers. Inefficient and over-staffed state-owned enterprises were the target of policy in the Fifteenth National Congress of 1997, leading to greater freeing up of public resources in order to establish a 'modern enterprise system', echoing the principle of 'holding on to large (state-owned enterprises) while letting the small go to market' (*zhuada fangxiao*). Within a few years policy makers had green lighted a plan for media conglomerates (*jituan*) which were intended to guarantee 'cultural security' (*wenhua anquan*). In effect, the discourse of cultural security was a precursor to China's succession to the World Trade Organization in 2001. While cultural security maintains some supporters, the other side of the coin is that China seeks to be a successful cultural exporter. It is perhaps significant that the term cultural security is not used in this book.

China's Tenth Five-Year Plan (2001–2005) signalled a new emphasis on raising productivity through technology and innovation. It was at this historical juncture, coterminous with China's accession to the World Trade Organization, that culture came to play a major development issue. During the ratification of the Tenth Five Year Plan the term 'cultural industries' (*wenhua chanye*) was formalized. The cultural industries had experienced a long gestation.[5] The commercial exploitation of cultural resources advocated by many reformers led to a rush of policy-making, often made on the run, by provincial and local governments anxious to find an appropriate 'cultural industry strategy'.

---

[5] Michael Keane, *Created in China: The Great New Leap Forward* (London: Routledge, 2007).

These developments were embedded in a larger development discourse. The Chinese national innovation strategy (NIS) was a response to a rising tide of international reports about knowledge-based economies, innovation as competitive advantage, and a shift in the world economy from goods to services, a world in which routine production of commodities was moving to the newly industrialized world. New supply chains emerged to exploit China's low cost economic development model. With China taking advantage of non-unionized labour to procure overseas contracts, factories proliferated, particularly in medium-sized Chinese cities.

It is at this point that we begin to pick up where Li Wuwei begins his narrative. China's focus on its low-cost manufacturing constitutes a central theme of the book's argument. According to Li, there is a saying:

They eat the meat and we eat the bone. They eat the rice and we eat the bran.

Li believes this illustrates the conundrum of 'Made in China'. Essentially, 'sweat industries' have been the reason for China's emergence as an economic hegemon.[6] Li argues that China's dependence on exports and low-cost processing, in effect its core economic model during the past two decades, has produced unwanted consequences. The desire to attract manufacturing to China, whether final products or 'trade in tasks', has generated widespread disregard for environmental protection and workplace safety. In many cases foreign companies have been complicit.

A similar view has been expressed on several occasions by Premier Wen Jiabao.[7] With over 80 per cent of China's GDP going to exports and fixed investment, and with export demand fluctuating in the wake of the financial crisis, China needs to have alternative development models. This is a powerful message of this book. Moreover, with costs rising in China's cities, low-end production has moved to less-expensive inland locations, and increasingly to third world countries including Africa, ironically a continent where China has provided much aid. In particular, China's large municipalities, now with an excess of unproductive factory space, have called for cleaner, greener solutions

---

[6] Li Wuwei, *Chuangyi gaibian Zhongguo* (Creative Industries are Changing China) (Beijing Xinhua Press, 2009).

[7] In March 2007 Premier Wen first raised the problem of the four 'uns' affecting China's economy: 'unbalanced, unstable, uncoordinated and unsustainable'. See Stephen Roach, *The Next Asia: Opportunities and Challenges for a New Globalization* (New Jersey: John Wiley and Sons, 2009, Introduction, p. xii).

to development. Li argues that China must find a new development model, a view supported by China's most eminent economic policy advisor, Hu Angang, from the Chinese Academy of Sciences.[8]

The Creative Industries come to China

The concept of the 'creative industries' has been the subject of much contestation and misunderstanding since its formulation by the British Department for Culture, Media and Sport (DCMS) in the late-1990s.[9] The definition is by now well known: 'activities that have their origin in individual creative skill and talent and which have the potential for wealth creation through the generation and exploitation of intellectual property.'[10] The DCMS nominated thirteen industry sectors; most have been accepted in countries where the idea has been picked up albeit with some degree of variation. One of the criticisms of the creative industries is that the concept is difficult to define: where does creativity begin and end for instance? Many of the policy arguments in support of the creative industries are premised on data that shows that they are the fastest growing segment of the economy.[11] This strength of argument relies on bundling; in other words, what is included in the mix. Different regions in China interpret the idea according to their needs and resources. In many cities, in particular Beijing, the concept has been expanded to include tourism; this considerably increases the value, the scale, and therefore the impact of the creative industries. In developed countries the emphasis is less on traditional culture, which is often seen as 'the cultural industries', and more on new media, user-created content and consumer productivity. In developed economies new media are the key drivers of the so-called 'creative economy'.

For some critics the creative industries idea is an expedient neo-liberal inversion of the term 'culture industry', coined by Horkhemier and Adorno in the 1940s. In this critical account culture had become administered,

---

[8] 'No redistribution, no *xiaokang*', Editorial *China Daily* Saturday October 16, 2010, p. 3.
[9] The original use of this term can be dated to the Australian Labor Party's cultural policy document, *Creative Nation*, 1994.
[10] DCMS Department for Culture, Media and Sport *Creative Industries Mapping Document*. DCMS: London, 1998.
[11] See John Howkins, *The Creative Economy: How People Make Money from Ideas* (London: The Penguin Group, 2002); also *The Creative Economy Report 2008*, UNCTAD Berne.

homogenous, subject to the forces of industrial capitalism.[12] For others, the 'creative industries' symbolizes a shift towards open innovation, a wiki-model of knowledge sharing in which citizen-consumers constantly rewrite the rules of creative engagement.[13] From this perspective the term 'industry' is far less visible and arguably increasingly redundant. Between control and openness, however, we note utilitarian definitions. Indeed, the creative industries are seen primarily as an economic development strategy in China and this constitutes one of the central themes of this book. Industrialization is seen as a positive force, as post-industrialization, namely the shift from 'Made in China' to 'Created in China'.[14] The theme of post-industrial society sits comfortably alongside the creative industries. There are similar ways of expressing the post-industrial economy; the US has long spoken of the 'entertainment industries' and the copyright industries while Japan and Korea now talk of the rising value of content industries.

The 'creative industries' initially found favour in the former colonial territories of Singapore and Hong Kong in 2003, before moving to Mainland China. As Li Wuwei describes in chapter one, the concept had its gestation in Shanghai in 2004. In 2004–2005, the first wave of international conferences on creative industries was held in Beijing[15] and Shanghai.[16] These are now annual events, combined with performances and business transactions. Li was, and remains the principal architect and proponent of this idea in China. By 2007,

---

[12] For an interesting revision and critique, see Scott Lash and Celia Lury, *Global Culture Industry: the Mediation of Things* (Cambridge: Polity, 2007).

[13] The research conducted by the Australian Research Council Centre of Excellence for Creative Industries and Innovation at the Queensland University of Technology focuses on the role that creative innovation plays in society. For information and publications see http://www.cci.edu.au/ [accessed 8 March 2011].

[14] The slogan was devised by a Beijing-based thinker Su Tong in 2004. See Keane, 2007 for a discussion of its inception.

[15] The conference was called The First International Creative Industries and Innovation Conference. Its theme was 'Creative Industries and Innovation in China'. The event was initiated by founding Dean John Hartley of QUT Creative Industries Faculty (see *International Journal of Cultural Studies*, volume 9 no 3, Sept 2006). It was co-sponsored by the Chinese Academy of Social Sciences (Prof. Zhang Xiaoming) and the Humanistic Olympics Research Centre of the Renmin University (Prof. Jin Yuanpu).

[16] The China Creative Industries Development Forum 2004 was held in Shanghai in Dec. 2004. Its theme was 'Creative Economy, leading China's Urban Development'. The first forum on creative industries was initiated by the Shanghai Academy of Social Sciences and Shanghai Theatre Academy, and was supported by the Shanghai Economic Commission, Publicity Department of Shanghai Municipality. Li Wuwei was the Chairperson of the conference.

the slogan 'From Made in China to Created in China' appeared in national and local press reports on the mainland.[17]

The question that Li investigates in this book is not whether creativity is changing China – but 'how creativity is changing China.' The book is organized according to its original purpose, to introduce the idea of the creative industries and to show how it is generating change not only in core cultural activities such as film, design and fashion, but how it facilitates innovation in other parts of the economy and in social relations. Li's development model describes a transformation from creative industries specifically to the creative economy, more generally and ultimately to the creative society.

The idea of creative industries is not a neutral concept in China. In order for it to be validated by the Ministry of Culture it has to connect with the policy mainstream. In effect, it has to coexist with the 'cultural industries', which is the 'industrial development' terminology favoured in Beijing. The term 'cultural creative industries', also used in Taiwan, is a means of compromising between two camps. The cultural industries are more directly associated with traditional culture and a conservative social agenda: that is, they are associated with cultural security more so than internationalization. In many places in China the terms cultural and creative industries are used interchangeably, depending on the audience of the day.

In this book there is an important distinction made between technological creativity and cultural creativity, although Li maintains the two are interdependent. Indeed, the conjoining of culture and creativity (in the term cultural creative industries) does reconcile with a traditional Chinese world view. According to David Hall and Roger Ames the Chinese metaphysical world is based on correlative thinking; for instance correlations between heaven (*tian*) and humanity (*ren*), between change (*bian*) and continuity (*tong*), between substance (*ti*) and function (*yong*). According to this world view, the well-known phrase 'as different as night and day' would be 'as different as night-becoming-day from day-becoming-night'.[18] Without wishing to essentialize what is a very significant policy moment, we might say the correlation we see today is one of 'culture-becoming-creativity' and 'creativity-becoming-culture'.[19]

---

[17] Michael Keane, *Created in China: the Great New Leap Forward* (London: Routledge, 2007).
[18] David Hall and Roger Ames, *Thinking from the Han: Self, Truth and Transcendence in Chinese and Western Culture.* (New York: SUNY Press, 1998, p. 127).
[19] For an extended discussion of this idea see Michael Keane, *China's New Creative Clusters: Governance, Human Capital and Investment* (London, Routledge, 2011).

In addition, the creative industries 'fit' the nation's attempt to refresh its image and to build international soft power. Li refers to the concept of 'cultural soft power'. This idea has come into the Chinese lexicon in recent years and its articulation into the cultural field is evident in the many policies that are attempting to increase the profile of Chinese culture, both nationally and internationally.

A Changing China

In the book we find many references to how creative industries function as a means of 'upgrading' China's economic structure, as well as society and people's values. Because Li is wearing four different 'hats' – economist, politician, researcher and independent thinker, the content is to a large extent instructional and the tone normative. The book is directed at the Chinese reader; it is meant to convince policy makers of the need to shift the development model from an export-driven model to a consumption-oriented one.

With Li being an industrial economist, we find a deal of emphasis on economic theory. As mentioned in the beginning of this introduction the concept of 'capital' informs mainstream Chinese economics; in the book these include intellectual capital, knowledge capital, social capital, consumer capital and cultural capital, all of which are metaphors on the notion of physical capital. The key idea is capital stock exists; this yields a rate of return and is subject to accumulation by investment. The role of policy is therefore to provide the right policy levers to allow the accumulation and the upgrading of the economy, to encourage investments in clusters and in infrastructure.

In economic theory this is essentially a neo-classical model with socialist underpinnings. The discussion of a creative economy does however allow a connection with a more Schumpeterian approach in which entrepreneurial activities change the value of various capital stocks, increasing the value of some and decreasing the value of others. This in turn generates structural change and produces uncertainty. Creative endeavours are based on uncertainty – that is, we generally don't know whether we like a cultural product until we consume it. While future return-on-investment is not so amenable to prediction this does not mean that the environment for creative activity cannot be planned. The term 'creative economy' therefore encapsulates a range of emerging organizational strategies and attempts to generate profit in clusters, bases, zones, quarters, and in new industry sectors where business models are untested.

In China the creative economy illustrates the aspirations of municipal and local governments to generate capital from the cultural market. Cultural policy is therefore closely aligned with economic growth theory, urban regeneration and local entrepreneurship. In this triangular relationship there is a sense that government must shoulder much of the responsibility for planning. As a result, there is recognition of the need for 'informed' top-down planning. This book provides a blueprint for how culture is being re-imagined in China.

Along with the policy task of prescribing solutions, Li raises critical issues in relation to the important question of tolerance. In particular, the final chapter addresses the challenge of promoting greater diversity. The message I believe is that the goal of a creative society cannot be achieved simply from the top down. A more comprehensive social transformation has to occur.

In the past few years hundreds of cultural and creative clusters have been built in China. Many of these are literally termed 'bases' (*jidi*) and provide the material infrastructure and space for the production of goods and services related to the cultural economy, such as animation, film and TV, fashion and industrial design. Some of these such as Beijing's 798 Art Zone and Shanghai's Tianzifang are internationally recognized; because they attract large numbers of visitors they are able to deliver quantifiable economic benefits. However, we are yet to know exactly how the majority are functioning. There are suggestions that many will not survive if they fail to deliver returns. Echoing Richard Florida's proposition that city growth strategies should be based on building communities that are attractive to creative people, Li Wuwei looks beyond the economics of clusters.[20] Li's advocacy of creative communities resonates with what many in the international community expect to see in an open society. His emphasis on 'social creativity' and 'creative communities' provide new ways to think about the situated nature of art, design, and media production in China. He talks frequently about 'borderless industries', about the need to understand how interactions between people contribute to the soft infrastructure of creativity.

For those unfamiliar with China's recent social reforms, the theme of diversity might appear a bit unusual. After all, the international media is

---

[20] Richard Florida, *The Rise of the Creative Class and How It's Transforming Work, Leisure, Community and Everyday Life* (New York: Basic Books, 2002).

quick to criticize China's reluctance to embrace Western-style democracy. Many in the international community, particularly commentators in liberal democracies, view the artist, the filmmaker, and the writer as a person who speaks 'uncomfortable truths'. However comparisons with Western liberal democracies often miss the great advances that have been made in China over the past decade or more. Frequent visitors to China will be aware of a changing China, a China where critical views can be expressed openly, albeit within limits. Writers are engaged in truth telling, in exposing the darker side of society. Filmmakers are exploring more sensitive issues. Artists are proliferating.

But the creative society comes with no guarantees of success; it thrives on constraints; we need creative ways to solve problems, but in the process this raises more questions. Ideally such a creative society reflects an open system model; overcoming one constraint leads to possibilities as well as new challenges. Creative destruction is something to be embraced not feared. In the creative economy inputs into one area change others, markets are volatile. There are other constraints, such as opportunity and transactions costs. Becoming a creative artist, or a creative entrepreneur, usually requires considerable investment in time, the process of developing one's skills in a particular domain that could be spent on other economic pursuits. In addition, the creative person often needs to compromise their output in order to get their work in the marketplace; for instance, they may need to avail themselves of agents and intermediaries.

The shift from 'Made in China' to 'Created in China' is underway, of this there can be no doubt. However, this is not a case of simply substituting one development model for another. As Richard Sennett has argued, 'making, whether this is basic manufacturing or the crafting of artefacts, depends on the development and refining of skills'.[21] These skills and techniques in turn develop through the powers of imagination, what we call creativity. To ensure that imagination and creativity work in tandem we need language expressed in various forms: debates, forums, written recipes, guide books and even chance encounters in tea (or coffee shops). Creative communities and 'communities of practice' are grassroots manifestations of social transformation in China. The language of policy makers is also important. In this regard, this book is a major achievement: it provides a compelling account of the nature of change in China.

[21] Richard Sennett, *The Craftsman* (London: Penguin Books, 2008).

Foreword

John Howkins

The surest way to self-fulfilment is to express one's personal creativity within a harmonious context. People have long known the wonderful excitement and immense satisfaction to be gained from using their individual creative imagination. It is a great joy to have one's own ideas, and express them in a group. It is a source of status and a boost to self-confidence. It is an essential step towards learning and personal development. Wherever the environmental conditions are right, people want to express themselves and solve problems.

Recently, we have discovered the practical value of creativity in social systems and in business. It is now recognized as a general factor in how we work together and in what we produce. This is the reason for its astonishing growth. It now operates on a vast scope and scale.

In some circles, creativity may be thought to be the exclusive privilege of the artist. This is not true. Surely, creativity is a universal aptitude, found in all children and available to all adults. Artists use their creativity in one way; scientists in another; investors in another; entrepreneurs in yet another. They are each wrestling with their imaginations to produce ideas that are better and more beautiful than what already exists and they already know.

The creative economy is therefore not another sector alongside agriculture, manufacturing and services but a transformation of all sectors. It transforms the ways in which all organizations acquire, use and trade ideas. Its principles hold true wherever people want to make their community, their work, their world, more fit for their purpose.

The result is a creative ecology based on cities with high energy: creative cities. We see the effects already. The media, design and entertainment industries whose products deal in intangible values have adjusted quickest to the new opportunities. Many companies that operated an innovation cycle once or twice a year now create new ideas continuously. Virgin and Google launch a new product every two weeks. Fashion retailers which previously scheduled two style seasons a year now change their designs every four weeks. Lego and BMW use the internet to invite comments on their products every day.

Most of these new ideas will fail. Failure is endemic in the creative economy. These companies exemplify economist Joseph Schumpeter's phrase about 'creative destruction', referring to the unavoidable need for continuous change and adaptation if an economy is to grow.

The most important factor in a creative economy is education. There is a high correlation between a country's education level and the size and strength of its creative economy. But we must be careful what we mean by 'education'. Education is useful only if it enables people to learn. Educating by instruction may be appropriate in some circumstances but it can stifle a person's capacity to learn. The short-term benefits can be outweighed by long-term damage. An education system that merely organizes the one-way delivery of facts does not help creativity. We need a system that provokes conversation, dialogue and thoughtfulness.

People have differing capacities to learn. We can also sense different capacities between communities and between cities. Creative people want to work where they can learn quickly from their peers and from the best in the field. Young people and people wanting jobs are attracted to cities where they can get work and where they can learn to get better at their work.

Truly creative people never stop learning. If they stop learning they die just as inevitably as a car without fuel will stop. This 'capacity to learn' is a useful principle. It is the hallmark of a creative company just as much as of a creative person. A good manager will ensure that everyone in the company is actively learning both for themselves and for the company. It affects both a company structure and the way people are managed. It affects innovation; research; sales. It is especially important in China's two-way relationship with other cultures.

The creative economy is best described as based on an attitude of mind that affects all sectors. The result transforms networks, technologies and consumer demand. The result is an improvement of people's lifestyle and quality of life. However, governments have to be careful to formulate the right policies. National and city governments need to ensure that their polices are appropriate or they will lose out culturally and economically.

The creative economy originated in Europe and America but is now seen as a worldwide phenomenon. Its shape in the twenty-first century will be profoundly affected by China. China's decisions on education and business in the coming years will have a major impact on how everyone worldwide sees culture, creativity and innovation. Everywhere people are asking, 'What is China's vision for the creative economy of the twenty-first century?'

I am honoured to write the foreword for this book for my friend and colleague Li Wuwei who has led China's understanding of the creative economy so wisely and skilfully. He reveals the scope of the creative economy from the arts to tourism and even agriculture. He is a powerful leader of these global developments. Li Wuwei is the best person to answer the question, 'What is China's vision of the creative economy?'

Preface

The Chinese edition of *How Creativity is Changing China* was written at a time when China was experiencing the thirtieth anniversary of its fast-moving economic reforms. It also coincided with the period of global economic recession brought about by America's economic crisis.

How has this crisis impacted on China's and the world economy?

For a long time the Chinese economy has been reliant on its natural resources and cheap labour. It has been export-oriented, its economy led by manufacturing.

What is the future direction of the Chinese economy in the twenty-first century? As an independent economist, a scholar who has researched creative industries for a long time, and as a person who provides specialist consultancy and advice for government ministries, I am pleased to observe that the Chinese economy has started a historical transition, one which will deliver great social change. The transition is closely related to creativity and innovation.

The concept of creative industries originated in the United Kingdom. It has spread within developed countries such as Australia, Japan and Korea. It has also been taken up enthusiastically in China, a country with a 5,000 year history and a splendid culture. Since 2004, the concept has spread quickly, challenging existing ways of doing things and old industrial models. Along with economic and social development, cultural and technological creativity is now playing a leading role in economic growth; these represent important indicators in measuring regional competitiveness as well as national soft power – on an individual, enterprise, economic and social level. In China the creative industries have facilitated innovation in the economic system; they have had positive effects on optimized industrial structures, and they have impacted on regional and national competitiveness.

In history, whether ancient or modern, eastern or western, whenever a great crisis occurs there is some form of transformation. In the Chinese language the word for crisis (*weiji*) is composed of two parts, one is *wei* which implies calamity or danger; the other part is *ji*, which refers to opportunity or a turning point. If a crisis is dealt with well, it can bring about transformation and things move onto a new stage.

During the Great Depression of 1929 the films of Charlie Chaplin had a therapeutic effect on people; at the time *Steamboat Willie* was a popular cartoon which resulted in the creation of Micky Mouse; the 'entertainment empires' Disney and 20th Century Fox were subsequently formed. In the 1970s the oil crisis led to the rise of the animation industry in Japan. The originality of these animations reflected unique aspects of Japanese culture. Japanese animation has enjoyed an increasing market in Asia and Europe. At the start of the twenty-first century, the nation began endeavouring to transform from a manufacturing model to a culture-export model. As a result, income from its animation industry now exceeds income from the auto industry. Following the 1990s financial crisis South Korea developed its content industries, notably electronic games and new media, culminating in the so-called 'Korean Wave' which has been highly influential in Asia.

In 2008–9 the force of the global financial crisis was felt all over the world; even China could not escape. China suffered a contraction in demand from the global market. Chinese exports fell quite severely, generating a production capacity surplus in many traditional industries; many businesses experienced financial hardship. The creative industries were able to emerge unscathed from the bad times, even finding new opportunities to develop. Their success lay in the fact that they promote economic innovation; they stimulate autonomous innovation in the traditional industries and, in doing so, they facilitate the transformation of the entire economic structure.

On the 25th September 2010, while on a visit to America, the Chinese Premier Wen Jiabao, gave a presentation entitled *Knowing the Real China* at a United Nations forum in which he said: 'China's modernization program now faces many unprecedented challenges: there are contradictions between progressive and backward, new and old.' Premier Wen spoke of the challenges and the contradictions: an increasingly strong economy but a deteriorating natural environment, a strong nation in terms of export but exports that were low in technology and value added. He noted that generally speaking, China is at the low end of the global industrial chain with over capacity in manufacturing. Its emerging industries lack innovation and creativity. The democratic system has yet to develop fully and social problems, such as injustice and corruption continue to exist.

In this book I have not commented at length on the problems currently facing China. I have used simple language in response to complicated questions.

I have advanced the proposition that the development of the creative industries will bring about the formation of a creative economy. This development will be followed by a third stage, the emergence of the creative society. These days China is still dealing with how to transform itself from the first stage in this process, from having creative industries to becoming a creative economy. The contribution of creative industries is primarily to use the attributes of high value adding and diffusion to stimulate the development of related industries and promote the upgrading of existing, more traditional industries.

A nation's level of industrial innovation and economic development go hand in hand. In 2009 per capita GDP in China reached US$3700. This compares with a figure of $US800 in the 1990s. The per capita GDP in 2009 of developed eastern cities like Shanghai, Beijing and Guangzhou has already passed $US10 000, reaching the level of relatively developed countries.

With economic development and an increase in salaries, people's livelihood has increased from the subsistence level of the last century to today's well-off, even affluent levels. The consumption of cultural and entertainment goods is increasing; people are more ready to participate in creative expression. Creativity and innovative technologies will continue to drive social progress in the coming decades.

Taking a longer view, creativity will change China! In this book I explore the concepts of 'borderless industries', the value system of creative industries, creative clusters, and creative communities. This book touches on ideas and concepts such as people's overall development, the profit model of enterprises, the upgrading of existing industries, and the comprehensive development of cities and a successful social ecology. In covering all this, the book provides a comprehensive interpretation of creative industries. It shows how they facilitate the transformation of both economy and society.

Of course, from the perspective of evolutionary economics, creative industries are constantly changing while playing a role in facilitating cultural, economic and social development. From a global perspective, creative industries have proved to be industries with high stakes; there is a relatively high rate of failure due to the existence of multiple uncertainties and unpredictable markets. Therefore, the encouragement of individual creativity and industrial innovation is not enough: there is a need to establish and implement a 'soft infrastructure' which includes enabling government policy, business support for creative enterprises, the cultivation of talent, the planning of environments conducive to creativity, the protection of intellectual property, investment and access to financial services. These are some of the huge challenges China is facing.

Li Wuwei

Acknowledgements

The rise of creative industries in China has not only received close attention and support from the Chinese government at all levels, but has aroused the attention of the international community. China's economic and social transformation from former industrial economy to creative economy has only recently begun. In the course of this long journey of transition, China will have to deal with all kinds of challenges, uncertainties and exciting changes, and I'm sure that creativity and innovation will be the core driving forces in this ongoing transformation. Since it was first published by Xinhua Press House in 2009, this book has been reprinted six times. Following the publication of a Korean edition, launched in Seoul in April 2010, I am very pleased that an English edition will be launched in London in 2011. A Japanese edition is scheduled to appear in 2011. I'm hoping that *How Creativity is Changing China* will provide readers with the perspective of a Chinese scholar, so that more people from home and abroad will understand the changes taking place, the critical problems China faces and the potential of its creative future.

The English edition of this book would not have been published without the support and assistance of the following people. First, I would like to thank Frances Pinter of Bloomsbury Academic for her constructive ideas and advice during the initial revisions of the Chinese edition. My special thanks go to the translation team: my old friend Professor Michael Keane and his research assistant Li Hui of Queensland University of Technology, Australia, Marina Guo of the School of Creative Studies, Shanghai Theatre Academy for their dedication and teamwork. The English translation, while loyal to the Chinese edition, is a work of both academic quality and readability. In the Editor's Introduction, Professor Keane offers critical interpretations and critiques based on personal research, long observation, and a deep understanding of the Chinese culture. In doing so, he provides a window through which foreign readers can better understand the future of Chinese culture and creativity, thereby contributing to international collaboration and exchange.

I would also like to express my heartfelt thanks to John Howkins, author of *The Creative Economy*. He wrote the foreword for this book, in which he offers his evaluation of the development of China's creative economy and makes some valuable suggestions. As always, he is full of hope for China.

While acknowledging the efforts in recent years by John Howkins and Professor Keane in propagating the idea of the creative economy and promoting the development of China's creative industries, I am very pleased to have the support of Distinguished Professor Stuart Cunningham, Director of the Australian Research Council's Centre of Excellence for Creative Industries and Innovation (CCI), Distinguished Professor John Hartley, Research Director of CCI, and Professor Justin O'Connor of the Creative Industries Faculty at Queensland University of Technology. Justin O'Connor and I have on many occasions exchanged ideas on the development of China's creative industries. John Hartley coined the concept 'the creative citizen' in his book *Creative Industries* (Blackwell Press 2005, Tsinghua University Press 2007), drawing a blueprint for the evolution of a creative society. Great minds think alike. I'm very pleased to acknowledge that Professor Hartley's model of the three phases of creative industries, from industries to economy to culture, or 'creative clusters, creative services, creative citizens' correlates positively with my own model of 'creative industries, creative economy, creative society'.

My thanks also go to my research team within the Research Centre for Creative Industries of the Shanghai Academy of Social Sciences: Wang Huimin, Wang Ruzhong, Wang Yumei, Yu Xuemei, Sun Jie and Jiang Lili. Without their dedication and support, this book would not have come to fruition. I would also like to express my special appreciation to my PhD student Marina Guo, who participated in the translation and editing of this book. During her visit to QUT as a recipient of an Australian Endeavour Research Award she worked hard and contributed a great deal to the English edition of this book, putting her skill for cross-cultural communication and her deep understanding of creative industries to good use.

Overseas publishing is an important step in realizing China's goal of 'culture going global.' In the publishing of this book, the Shanghai International Cultural Trading Promotion Committee and the Xinhua Press have given full support in terms of funding and copyright. Thanks are due to Zhang Chunsheng and Sun Huiding for their effective guidance in these matters.

The theory and practice of creative industries is maturing along with economic development and social progress. The development of China's creative industries needs the support and contribution of various communities. This book is dedicated to everyone who takes an interest in China's development.

Li Wuwei
March 2011
Beijing, China

Introduction

As an economist I pay close attention to current economic development and social issues. I continue to engage in research on industrial economics and economic management. I have published many influential theoretical papers in addition to providing policy advocacy. Apart from being a scholar, I have several responsibilities and professional activities: I am Vice Chairman of the National Committee of the 11th Chinese People's Political Consultative Conference (CPPCC), Vice Chairman of the Central Committee of the Chinese Kuomintang Revolutionary Committee, President of the Shanghai Creative Industries Association, and Director of the Research Centre for Creative Industries at Shanghai Academy of Social Sciences (RCCI SASS).

In recent years I have become particularly passionate about creative industries. As the term is still relatively new, many people in China do not have a clear idea of what the future might hold. I am pleased to be able to make a contribution to greater understanding by publishing this book.

Creative industries value innovation and individual creativity; they emphasize the importance of culture and art in economic development. The term can be traced to November 1998 when the British Ministry of Culture, Media and Sport released the *Creative Industries Mapping Document*. This document officially defined the concept and nominated sectors associated with creative industries.

After the 1997 British general election, Prime Minister Tony Blair initiated the idea of a 'new Britain', hoping to change the image of Britain as an old industrial empire. Sectors such as industrial design and art design were accorded a high status.

What does 'creative industries' mean? Are they in fact industries? There is still some controversy among academics. Some believe that creativity can be traced to ancient times and that it is almost impossible to categorize. Some consider creative industries are the same as 'cultural industries' and it is just a matter of terminology. In 1998, the United Kingdom Creative Industries Task Force provided the following definition:

> those industries which have their origin in individual creativity, skill and talent and which have a potential for wealth and job creation through the generation and exploitation of intellectual property.[1]

The concept was adopted within a few years in Singapore, Australia, New Zealand, and Hong Kong. There are differences across sectors, however, and in the activities that creative industries actually represent. These differences are reflected in policies and government statistics. The thirteen sectors categorized in the United Kingdom have been adopted in most countries and regions. These include advertising, architecture, the arts, the antique market, computer and video games, crafts, design, designer fashion, film and video, music, the performing arts, publishing, software, television and radio.

Urban transformation, increasing consumption, and technological advances are elements contributing to the rise of creative industries. In knowledge-based economies creativity represents an important force for global change. In the transition from industrial society to post-industrial society, the economic structure of cities is transforming from a focus on manufacturing to a focus on services and innovation. This urban transformation not only provides the soil for the sowing of creative industries but also investment and a sound environment for further development.

The increasing amount of time people spend on leisure pursuits has led to a growth in demand. Various kinds of cultural and creative products enjoy an ever-growing community of consumers. As demand for such goods and services becomes more individualized and diversified, the market responds with innovative solutions in terms of design, advertising and marketing. The development of creative industries not only satisfies cultural needs but expands them. In turn, this expansion of demand provides a solid social foundation and broader market space for the development of creative industries.

New technologies and the development of modern industries have made a huge impact on traditional art forms; the MP3 format, for instance, has changed the music recording industry and web publishing. Technology has assisted traditional art forms, as can be seen from the digitalization of various

---

[1]DCMS Department for Culture, Media and Sport *Creative Industries Mapping Document*. DCMS: London, 1998.

creative industries. Technology has in turn created a large number of new art forms and opened up new areas for development. Virtual space has changed the way in which people communicate, engage in activities and consume.

If we say that the manufacturing industries have made important contributions to the rapid development of the Chinese economy in the past thirty years, then it is not an understatement to say that in the next thirty years, cultural creativity and technological innovation will be key forces in bringing comprehensive changes in China's transition to an innovative society. The fact that creative industries are becoming a new engine for social and economic development has strategic significance for a Chinese economy confronted with a wide range of international and domestic challenges.

How is Creativity Changing China?

By developing creative industries individual creativity is nurtured. Moreover, creative industries are beneficial in maintaining and protecting historical and cultural heritage, improving cultural capital, and fostering communities. This leads to the improvement of the cultural assets of cities, the establishment of city brands and identity, the promotion of the creative economy, and overall economic and social development. It is in this context that creativity is changing China.

I consider two important kinds of creativity in this book: cultural creativity and technological innovation. They can be likened to the 'wheels of a cart and wings of a bird' for economic growth. Creative industries promote the transformation of the economic development model through transformation of resources, value upgrading, structural optimization, and market expansion.

- Transformation of resources: Creative industries turn various natural and cultural, tangible and intangible resources into capital for economic development. At the same time, they promote the transformation of various kinds of capital (economic, cultural and social).

- Value upgrade: R&D, design, sales, branding and services are the key links to increasing industry value added and to bringing about a transformation from 'Made in China' to 'Created in China.'

- Structural optimization: Creative industries optimize the structure of traditional cultural industries by re-creating and re-upgrading the resources of these industries. In addition, creative industries optimize the structure of primary, secondary and tertiary industries.

- Market expansion: The cultural features contained in a product can help the product to increase its value, and therefore sales, and to target a more diverse range of consumer demographics.

Many cultural and creative industries cluster in old factories and old warehouses. This kind of 'new ideas in old factories' model is a catalyst for urban development. It brings economic and social benefits. The secret to success is not simply relying on favourable policies to attract foreign business and capital, building various kinds of large factory precincts, and promoting the development of science and technology. There needs to be a shift of attention from 'materials' to 'people': that is, to attract creative talent and build creative communities.

The development of creative industries requires the participation of social institutions and non-profit organizations; for instance, the development of Shanghai's creative industries is not due solely to government behaviour. Neither is it due to pure market behaviour. It is the result of a joint effort by the government, the market and intermediary institutions; that is, it is driven by all three forces. To be specific, it is coordinated by the Shanghai Creative Industries Association, operated by the Shanghai Creative Industries Centre, and supported in terms of theoretical research by the Research Centre for Creative Industries, SASS.

Established in August 2005, the Shanghai Creative Industries Association is a non-profit, cross-sector and cross-ownership organization. It provides creative industries-related policy consultancy and advice for the government. It integrates resources, gathers talent and establishes exchange platforms. It assists the government in making (or rectifying) policies, regulations, and standards and pushes for their implementation. It provides market services for its members through cooperative projects, consultancy and training, intermediary services, conferences and exhibitions, and publishing and distribution. It plays an important role in promoting the healthy development of Shanghai's creative industries.

The Shanghai Creative Industries Centre, was established in November 2004 and was officially operational in January 2005. It is a platform for the practice and operation of Shanghai's creative industries. It is also an intermediary organization for enterprise development. It aims at taking advantage of all social resources to assist government in working out development plans and strategies. It plays the role of industry guidance and promotes creative clusters. It promotes the overall development of Shanghai's creative industries by mobilizing enterprises and talent.

The Research Centre for Creative Industries SASS was established in September 2004. It is one of China's first research institutions for creative industries. Its *Creative Industries* journal and *Creative Industries China* (www. cncti.org.cn) website are authoritative exchange platforms for China's creative industries. As a leader in creative industries theory, the centre associates the development of cultural and creative industries with the transformation of the economic development model, the upgrade of the industrial structure, the improvement of regional competitiveness and the building of city brands. Its research focuses on the development of creative industries, regional innovation, creative cities, creative tourism, innovation in business administration and industrialization models. It provides academic arguments for the development of Shanghai's creative industries.

As the concept of creative industries was coined in the middle of the 1990s and was only introduced to China in recent years, a considerable number of people are still unfamiliar with it. This can generate confusion. At present, China's creative industries are still at the initial development stage and there is still much to do before cities become capable of integrating resources and accumulating capital for development. Moreover, development in China is still at the industry level; the role of creative industries in promoting economic development, bringing about innovation in other economic fields and stimulating coordinated social development is not fully demonstrated yet. The creative economy will undergo a long development process for the formation of the creative economy, ranging from talent cultivation to urban transformation. It requires vision. It requires adaptation to developments in the global economy. It requires confidence in our own developmental advantages. It requires us to put a high priority on those industries that will make important contributions to China's economic growth and coordinated social development in the future.

Backed up by 5,000 years of Chinese civilization and increasingly dynamic creative potential, China is determined to develop into a creative nation with global influence.

Creativity is changing China: that is an ideal for the nation; it is also a reality.

1

China's Creative Power

China's Creativity on the World Stage

When David Beckham kicked a soccer ball towards a cheering audience at the closing ceremony of the 2008 Beijing Olympic Games, this symbolic gesture created a link between the Olympic cities of Beijing and London. Broadcast across the world it was an invitation to the London Olympic Games.

The 2008 Beijing Olympic Games provided a showcase for China's creativity. The opening ceremony was directed by the world-renowned film director Zhang Yimou and used art, culture and technology to represent a coming together of history and modernity. On a large LED scroll digital images slowly unfurled, illustrating the path of Chinese civilization. As the cauldron was lit, Olympic gymnast Li Ning ran along the upper wall of the stadium. A digital scroll opened in front of him showing footage of previous torch relays.

At the Shanghai World Expo in 2010 the city was characterized as an Eastern Pearl. Website visitors enjoyed an interactive experience featuring 3D and virtual reality. The common link between the Opening Ceremony of the Beijing Olympic Games and the Shanghai World Expo website was a company specializing in 3D visualization technology. The company was Crystal.

Crystal was established in 1995. At the time it was a small studio of a few dozen employees providing architectural visualization services. Crystal was fortunate to begin its growth during a strong period of economic development. It has since grown into the largest enterprise of its kind in Asia offering film and television special effects, 3D animation, multimedia, and 3D image exhibition. Crystal now employs over 3,000 people with eight branches globally. In March 2009, Crystal became the official computer graphics (CG) service provider for the 2012 London Olympics and Paralympics Games. So far, it is the only Chinese enterprise to provide support for the London Olympics. 'What is most exciting and unique about this industry is being able to integrate the charm of technology with artistic creativity and then to carry out commercial operations,' said Lu Zhenggang, founder of Crystal.

Made in China

'They eat the meat and we eat the bone. They eat the rice and we eat the bran.' This apt description reminds us that the Made in China phenomenon is founded on 'sweat industries.' 'Made in China' and 'created by foreign capital' now symbolize competition among nations for China's low cost resources.

Due to changing patterns in industrial production over the past two decades, China has welcomed manufacturing industries formerly concentrated in Europe, the United States, Japan and other developed regions. 'Made in China' products now appear in every corner of the world. China has become a 'world factory.' Nevertheless, it should be acknowledged that 'Made in China' has been an important driver of China's economic growth and in turn this model has made significant contributions to the world economy. IMF statistics reveal that China's GDP in 2008 was the third highest in the world.[1] But GDP by itself means neither wealth nor happiness; nor does it mean ecological sustainability. China's economic growth has relied largely on investment and export, giving rise to problems such as exhaustion of natural resources, environmental pollution and lack of innovation. Behind the apparent dynamism of 'Made in China' is a huge loss of profits for Chinese enterprises.

A transition from 'Made in China' to 'Created in China' is the future strategy for China's economy.

But why do we need the change from 'Made in China'?

Let's look at the case of Logitech. In 2004, The *Wall Street Journal* reported that Logitech, a Swiss-American joint venture based in California, was the world's leading computer mouse manufacturer. In 2004, 20,000 PC mouses bearing 'Made in China' labels were exported to America. These were all assembled in Suzhou, China.

In 2004, the Wanda wireless mouse, one of Logitech's best-selling products, sold for US$40 in the US. Out of this retail price, Logitech took away US$8 (20 per cent), while distributors and retailers got US$15 (37.5 per cent), and component suppliers such as TI received US$14 (35 per cent).[2] The Suzhou

---

[1] IMF World Economic Outlook Databases, April 2009 Edition. International Monetary Fund. http://www.imf.org/external/data.htm [accessed 8 March 2011].

[2] Andrew Higgins, 'As China Surges, It Also Proves a Buttress to American Strength'. *Wall Street Journal*, January 30, 2004, Available at http://online.wsj.com/article/SB107542341587316028. html by subscription.

factory was left with just US$3 (7.5 per cent). Workers' pay, electricity, transportation and other overheads all had to come out of that $3. Moreover, the payroll of the 450 employees at Logitech's sales and marketing division in Fremont California is considerably higher than the total salaries of the 4,000 Chinese workers in the Suzhou factory. The *Wall Street Journal* article described the Suzhou workshop of Logitech as an illustration of the current world economy.

The Barbie Doll, popular on the American market, is Disney's best-selling brand toy for children. It is also manufactured in Suzhou by an original equipment manufacturer (OEM).[3] The retail price for this product in the US market is $10 while the FOB costs were $2.[4] Of the $2, $1 is for management and transportation fees, leaving $0.65 for cost of supplied materials and only $0.35 gross profit for the manufacturer in China.

What does this mean for Suzhou, one of China's export manufacturing bases? It sounds impressive to be an export manufacturing base with the advantage of foreign exchange incomes. But the reality is that while Suzhou has attracted a lot of foreign investment and claims rapid GDP growth, the growth of per capita income is much lower than that of GDP. Local people have not benefited much from the foreign investment and economic growth. In fact in relative terms they have become poorer.

China's manufacturing enterprises can be described as a coolie: he sweats over what he is making and sells it to the rich at a very low price. He uses the little money he makes to buy bonds from the rich. But the rich person is still not happy, criticizing him for working too hard without paying due attention to his health, making so much pollution that his home is no longer a safe place to live and taking away jobs from other people. Meanwhile, the rich person pays the poor guy principal and interest with a continuously devaluing currency. Liang Congjie, a well-known environmental expert, has an apt metaphor for this. He describes China as the world's kitchen and the world's swill bucket. We cook our best dishes and put them on the dinner table of the world for foreigners to enjoy. But the rubbish left from the

---

[3] An original equipment manufacturer, or OEM, manufactures products or components that are purchased by a company and retailed under the purchasing company's brand name.
[4] FOB specifies which party (buyer or seller) pays for which shipment and loading costs, and/or where responsibility for the goods is transferred.

preparation of that food is left behind in our own kitchen and in our own swill bucket.

The cases of Logitech and Barbie Doll reveal a sad and distressing dimension to China's manufacturing industries. The economist Jeffrey Sachs[5] says that he can understand why China has been able to maintain a 9 per cent plus growth rate for so long. Work in China takes place 24/7 rotating around machines, supporting the US economist Paul Krugman's opinion that the East Asian economy relies more on 'sweat' than 'ideas' to achieve growth.[6]

Someone once described foreign investors in China as follows: their investment accounts for 30 per cent of the capital; they own 50 per cent of the company shares; and they take away 70 per cent of the profit.[7] In the OEM model of production foreign investors can take up to 92 per cent of the profit. This is the face of 'Made in China' – it has a forced smile. If we do not transition to a 'Created in China' model and if we do not have our own intellectual property and innovative technology we will find ourselves in great danger. If foreign capital were to leave China on a large scale and if the economy was profoundly affected by another international financial crisis, what might be left to China except rundown factory buildings, polluted land and low-skilled workers? What else could China rely on to maintain its economic growth?

Created in China

As an ancient civilization, China is rich in cultural resources. Through creative development, these resources can be turned into products and services with a high cultural element. They can be transformed from cultural resources to economic resources. In addition, these 'creative industries' can stimulate consumption, expand domestic demand and generate more wealth and employment while playing a key role in communicating new ideas, enhancing the quality of public culture and promoting human development.

[5] Jeffrey D. Sachs and Wing Thye Woo 'China's Economic Growth After WTO Membership,' *Journal of Chinese Economic and Business Studies*, Vol. 1, No. 1, 2003, pp. 1–31.
[6] Paul Krugman, 'The Myth of Asia's Miracle,' *Foreign Affairs*, pp. 62–78. Available at http://www.pairault.fr/documents/lecture3s2009.pdf [accessed 15 April 2011].
[7] Yueren Wu (2005). 'Offshore Profit: Will China's Economy follow the Footprint of Latin America?' *China Market*. Vol. 7, 2005, p. 28.

The Creative Economy

Creative industries now assume a very important position within the global economy. The 'creative economy', a term that has come into widespread use, has the potential to generate exports, expand employment and increase income. At the same time it can promote social cohesion, cultural diversity and human development. The creative economy has become a strategic choice for many countries. For developing countries creative industries are regarded as an effective way to achieve 'leap frog' development as well as a successful strategy to transform existing modes of economic development. The United Nations Conference for Trade and Development (UNCTAD) believes that creative industries have advantages over other industries when it comes to achieving rapid growth for developed countries. *The Creative Economy Report 2008* by UNCTAD argues that creative industries are the new driving engine for global trade.[8]

According to the British government's *Creative Industries Mapping Document*, first released in 1998, the creative industries are:[9]

> those industries which have their origin in individual creativity, skill and talent and which have a potential for wealth and job creation through the generation and exploitation of intellectual property.[10]

At the core of these industries is the creativity of individuals. Individual talent and skill are seen as the drivers of economic growth and wealth accumulation. What is more significant, however, is that people have opportunities to give free rein to their creative abilities. Once stimulated, this becomes a powerful force and has the potential to change China's economic development model.

Creative industries are gaining momentum in China. In the wake of China's integration into the global economy, regional development is occurring in many parts of China. In these regions creativity is changing China's established management models and reforming ways of thinking.

[8] UNCTAD Creative Economy Report 2008, UNCTAD Berne: Switzerland.
[9] http://www.culture.gov.uk/what_we_do/creative_industries/default.aspx [accessed 15 April 2011].
[10] http://webarchive.nationalarchives.gov.uk/+/http://www.culture.gov.uk/reference_library/publications/4632.aspx [accessed 8 March 2011].

I once proposed[11] that the development of creative industries should be included in the state's plans for innovation and the state should implement policies related to them. We need to create an enabling and tolerant cultural atmosphere and encourage the development of non-profit organizations in the creative industries. As I discuss in the next chapter the development of creative industries has not only helped the economy out of financial crisis, but has helped to transform the economic development model into something more innovative. In a word, creative industries provide an effective roadmap to economic transformation in China.

Britain and Australia were pioneers in the creative industries. In 1994, Australia's cultural policy under the Labor Party recognized the concept of a 'creative nation'; in 1998, New Labour in Britain introduced specific policies relating to cultural industries. With the acceleration of globalization and information technology, developed countries have transformed their economies. The key elements that drive growth have undergone structural change; in turn culture and creativity are contributing increasingly to economic development. The development agenda initiated by creative industries has opened a window for global economic development, enabling us to see a new way to follow emerging development patterns, to come to terms with new key growth elements and to construct new industries in the current global economic, technological and cultural environment.

The extent of the creative economy is shown by the export vitality of creative products and services in developing economies. World Bank statistics show that the value created by the global creative economy in 2005 accounted for 6.1 per cent of the total volume of the world economy. Some estimates[12] suggest that the global revenue of core creative industries will reach US$4,100 billion by 2010 and US$8,000 billion by 2020.[13] The projected market expansion is providing China with opportunities.

---

[11] Wuwei Li (2009) 'Thoughts about The Development of Cultural and Creative Industries in China,' *Guangming Daily*, China: Nov. 23, 2009. Available at http://theory.people.com.cn/GB/10426655.html [accessed 8 March 2011].

[12] John Howkins. 'The Global Creative Economy 2000–2015'. ICEC International Creation and Economic Centre. http://www.icecngo.org/tourga/abc17.html [accessed 8 March 2011].

[13] The estimation is based on *The Global Creative Economy 2000–2015* by John Howkins: 'The core creative industries account for $2,900 billion ($2.9 trillion) worldwide. They are growing by about 7 per cent a year, If we project this 7 per cent growth rate into the future we can forecast that by 2010 they will account for $4,100 billion. By 2015 they will account for $5,775 bn and by 2020 as much as $8,100 bn.'

Creative Industries in China

Creative industries in China took root in Shanghai. The 'Shanghai Creative Industries Development Forum 2004', the first of its kind in China, marked the beginning.[14] It was the introduction to China, from concept to practice, of the creative industries. In my keynote speech I proposed that creative industries should be listed as strategic pillar industries in Shanghai's new round of development. I argued that a cross-departmental, cross-sector coordination mechanism should be implemented and that to optimize the industrial structure of Shanghai and to increase the city's competitiveness, development should be closely related to the preparation of the Shanghai Expo and the building of an international metropolis. In 2005, the Shanghai municipal government issued policies to stimulate the development of creative industries. Creative industries were also written into the *2005 Work Report of Shanghai Municipality* and the *Shanghai Cultural Development Plan for 2004–2010*.[15] A number of related social organizations and institutions were established. I was elected, and still am, the founding president of the Shanghai Creative Industries Association, which was established in 2005. The Shanghai Creative Industries Centre and the Shanghai Creative Industries Investment Co. Ltd were established and Shanghai's first batch of eighteen creative clusters was launched. The Research Centre for Creative Industries of Shanghai Academy of Social Sciences, China's first academic research institution in creative industries, and the School of Creative Studies of Shanghai Theatre Academy, a centre from which to nurture creative talent, were also established. These institutions collaborate with each other and effectively promote an integrated model of government, industry, education and research. In the five years from 2004 to 2009, the contribution of creative industries to the city's GDP accounted for 7.66 per cent, up from 5 per cent;[16] it had already become one of Shanghai's key pillar industries.

Following the first use of the term 'cultural industries' in a central government document in 2006 many plans were formulated in cities across

---

[14] This was held in December 2004 in Shanghai.

[15] Zhu Guang, 'Shanghai Creative Industries Association is established at Shanghai Theatre Academy.' *Xinmen News*, 17 Aug 2005. http://ent.sina.com.cn/x/2005-08-17/1825813195.html [accessed 8 March 2011].

[16] Shanghai Economic Commission, Shanghai Creative Industries Cluster Conference, Oct. 13, 2009. Shanghai, China.

China.[17] 'Creative Industries' became one of the ten popular phrases in China's mainstream media in 2006, a year that became referred to as 'the first year of China's creative industries.'[18] Creative industries have experienced solid growth due to support from national and municipal governments that have not only issued a series of policies, but have proposed ways in which cultural resources should be developed through science and technology and traditional cultural industries might be transformed and improved.

The Age of 3G

In January 2009, China's 'big 3' mobile communication operators, China Mobile, China Telecom and China Unicom, acquired third-generation (3G) mobile communication licenses. 3G has released the potential of the mobile

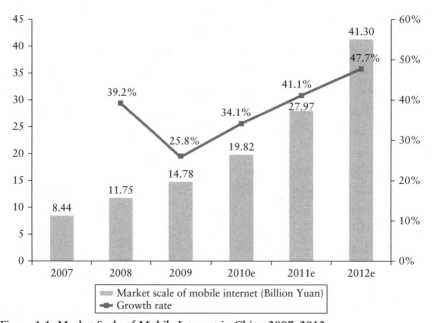

Figure 1.1 Market Scale of Mobile Internet in China 2007–2012
Source: based on a financial report of listed companies, industry data gathered from interviews and iResearch statistical models and estimates

---

[17] The *National 11th Five-Year Plan for Cultural Development*. In this document the actual term used was cultural industries.
[18] Jingcheng Zhang (ed.) *Chinese Creative Industries Report (2006)*. (Beijing: China Economic Publication House, 2006).

internet. From 2009 to 2010, China's direct investment in 3G was approximately RMB 280 billion. According to statistics from IResearch Consulting, the market scale of mobile internet in 2009 was RMB 14.78 billion, up 25 per cent from the previous year.[19]

Mobile internet provides a platform for demonstrating creativity. 3G content, especially content customized for users, relies largely on cutting-edge technology. For example, GPS technology makes it possible for the user to connect a mobile phone with an electronic map. Interactive games have huge market potential. Value-added mobile services are extending into all areas of social life, demonstrated by mobile streaming media, mobile e-commerce, mobile UGC and wireless sensing applications. Diversified innovative functions are providing convenient services in everyday life, business and finance.

The creation and communication of personalized content to a large extent relies on interaction between consumers and producers. This trend is best illustrated by mobile user-generated content (UGC) services. The user is not simply a consumer of web content: he or she is also a producer of the content. UGC allows the user to both download and upload. In the age of 3G, mobile UGC services, such as mobile blogging, mobile video and mobile communities, provide opportunities for the application of multimedia, in the form of images, music and video. In addition, the development of mobile payment services demonstrates the further integration of mobile industries with financial industries.

China's Creative Enterprises

According to the *Development Report of China's High-growth Creative Industries Enterprises 2009* released by CIDA (China Industrial Design Association) Creative Industries Assessment Centre, creative industries in China are mainly distributed across design services, web games, web and computer services, news and publishing, broadcasting, film and television, advertising and exhibition, animation, leisure and entertainment.

China's creative enterprises mainly consist of small- or medium-sized enterprises (SMEs); most are at the development stage, characterized by limited

---

[19] Source: Chinese Ministry of Industry and Information Technology, Statistic Data 2010. Available at http://finance.qq.com/a/20100111/003623.htm [accessed 8 March 2011].

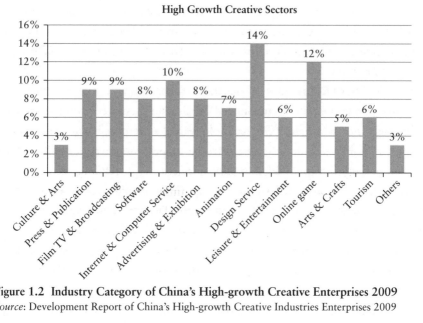

Figure 1.2 Industry Category of China's High-growth Creative Enterprises 2009
Source: Development Report of China's High-growth Creative Industries Enterprises 2009

capital and a small number of employees. There are no uniform criteria yet for the classification of such enterprises although the Beijing municipal government has its own guidelines; namely, small and medium-sized cultural and creative enterprises should meet the following criteria: 1) a registered capital of no less than RMB 300,000; 2) no more than 300 employees; 3) annual sales of no more than RMB 40 million. Among the 100 high-growth creative enterprises under survey, 64.7 per cent meet the criteria and 55 per cent have less than 100 employees.[20]

Despite the fact that China is a latecomer and that there are large regional differences, the sector is characterized by rapid high growth. The CIDA Creative Industries Assessment Centre survey shows that since 2006 China's creative enterprises achieved an average revenue growth of over 60 per cent for four consecutive years (2006–2009). In 2007, creative enterprises experienced explosive growth, over 97.43 per cent in average annual business revenue. In 2008, when the global financial crisis hit China, creative enterprises still maintained

---

[20] China's High-Growth Creative Enterprise Report, 2009. CIDA Creative Industries Assessment Centre, Report released at The 4th China Creative Industry Award & Summit, Beijing China. Nov. 2009. Available: http://www.techweb.com.cn/commerce/2009-11-27/482707.shtml [accessed 8 March 2011].

their growth, with high-growth creative enterprises achieving a growth of around 80 per cent. Since 2008, creative enterprises in general have improved their profit-making ability. The survey shows that in the 2006–2009 period, China's creative enterprises achieved positive growth with average business net profit reaching over 30 per cent in 2009.[21] The strong performance was probably a result of the following factors: first, national and municipal policies were issued and improved; second, there was increasing consumption of popular culture stimulated by the global financial crisis; and third, creative enterprises' low reliance on cost enabled them to suffer less from the economic downturn.

Successful creative enterprises need to be not only creative in products and services but also innovative in business models. Among the many Chinese creative enterprises, A8 Music is a good example. A8 Music obtains music content through www.a8.com [accessed 8 March 2011], a mature UGC original music interactive platform, and through licensing from domestic and international music companies. It promotes and sells the content through new media and traditional media such as the internet and a range of wireless networks. Through its integrated marketing and multi-channel distribution network, A8 Music collects information about user preferences and then works out personalized marketing strategies targeting different regions. The 'A8 Mobile Music Solution' is a multi-functional music service system that is delivered across multiple platforms of cable and wireless and which integrates music downloads, online listening, genre search, one-stop value-added services, music consultation, personalized user analysis, and cross-media music synchronization between mobile phone and PC. The innovation lies in the elimination of platform restrictions for music services. The user can easily and conveniently enjoy the best, the latest and most personalized integrated music services.

A8's success has come from focusing on the final link in the creative industries value chain. The chain runs from an original idea, to production, commercialization (e.g. exhibition, promotion, circulation and trade), following which there is extension of the chain, such as development, production and marketing of 'spin-off' products. A8 Music has implemented the 'one source, multi-use' strategy. A8 combines original music content with new media resources and explores multiple application channels such as B2B and B2C.

---

[21] China's High-Growth Creative Enterprise Report 2009. CIDA Creative Industries Assessment Centre, China, Nov. 2009.

Table 1.1 Comparison of the A8 Music Solution and a Traditional Music Production Company

	Traditional Music Production	A8 Music Solution
Industry Form	• investment in original music • promotion of musicians and performers • production and distribution of audio-visual products	• integration of music resources • use of intellectual property rights • a full range of digital music services
Resource	Single use	Repeatable use
Product Line	• audio-visual products • traditional media • traditional consumers	• music service • mobile phone, internet • new media clients
Industrial Chain	• linear production chain • focus on upstream original creation and production	• circle value chain • focus on downstream multi-platform distribution
Industrial Organization	• vertical structure • product-oriented	• flat structure • service-oriented
Orientation	Product value	Consumer value
Strategy	• competition – Red Ocean • promotion, expansion of product sales	• value creation – Blue Ocean • development of multiple wireless value-added services
Revenue	• increasing marginal cost • diminishing marginal revenue	• diminishing marginal cost • increasing marginal revenue

The key to A8's profit model is to understand that creative industries operate without borders. In terms of organizational form, creative industries break the boundaries of traditional industries, sometimes integrating with different

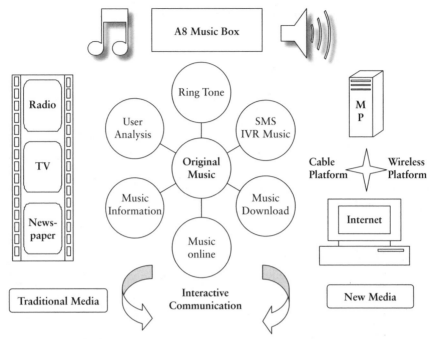

Figure 1.3 A8 Music Box

industries altogether. They provide coordinating services for other industries; for example, music content is a core product, yet it is used in other industries as an input factor, providing value-added functions for smartphones like Dopod, LG and Samsung. This is a good example of platform convergence in cable and wireless that allows interactivity between traditional and new media.

Smiling Curve

Smiling Curve theory[22] is often mentioned in the research of value chains. Drawing a line through the process of an industrial chain from the perspective of value added presents an arc curve that looks like a smiling face, with each end of the curve representing higher value added and the middle part lower

[22] The Smiling Curve term was originally proposed by Stan Shih, chairman of the Taiwan-based Acer Inc, to describe U-shaped profitability. http://en.wikipedia.org/wiki/Smiling_Curve [accessed 8 March 2011].

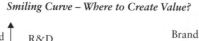

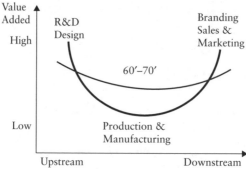

Figure 1.4 Smiling Curve

value added. In fact, the so-called Smiling Curve is a 'curve of value added': one end represents R&D and design and the other sales, branding and services while the middle part of the curve is manufacturing. Generally speaking, profit margin at both ends is between 20 per cent and 25 per cent whereas that of the manufacturing element in the middle is only 5 per cent.

At the left end of the Smiling Curve (the upstream of the value chain), value added increases in accordance with investment in R&D and design. At the right end (the downstream of the value chain), value added also increases in accordance with improvements in branding, sales channels and services. The manufacturing link, which produces the lowest value added of the whole industry value chain, is confronted with problems such as low technology, limited profit margins, fierce market competition and likelihood of being replaced by peers who can run at an even lower cost. This explains why a 'Made in China' Barbie Doll can only produce $1 in value for its manufacturer.

The value of both ends of the curve is mainly produced by creative industries which are positioned in the high ends of the value chain. A cultural idea can enter the market directly and realize value as merchandise. It can also create new related values. An example is the Yangzi River delta near Shanghai, which is undergoing structural readjustment. Having served for a long time as the growth 'engine' of the region, manufacturing industries are now 'contracting due to a series of readjustment policies and measures.' The change in their growth patterns needs the support of modern service industries. Cultural industries and other related sectors such as industrial design, advertising and exhibition, and animation merchandising are now playing a key role in development. Cultural industries stimulate consumption of cultural products while related industries produce unlimited output value.

China is now at a crucial historical moment. Over the years, China has developed into a manufacturing power and the world's factory. After achieving a certain degree of economic accumulation, this direction and approach of economic growth need to be re-examined closely in the light of current conditions. China used to be a labour-intensive, resource-exhausting and low-value-added manufacturing power with a lack of core technology and an imbalanced ecological system. China is confronting a series of social problems as a result of this. How can we avoid 'championing growth without development'? Given time, what will China become in the future?

How is creativity changing China? The way out of the current situation requires transformation. The *Creative Economy Report 2008* by UNCTAD points out that China may become the biggest nation of creative industries in the world (irrespective of controversy over statistics). China has vast potential in the high-value-added creative economy. Realizing this potential, however, requires Chinese enterprises to take the creative industries approach and to produce more value by moving up towards both high ends of the value added in the Smiling Curve. By doing so, China can expect to change its former position at the low end of the global industry value chain. The transformation from 'Made in China' to 'Created in China' will give Chinese enterprises a happier smiling face.

Cultural Productivity

As problems of economic development and the need to feed the population are solved, demand for cultural goods is increasing. Consumers want products to contain more cultural elements. The functional or 'use value' of consumer goods is no longer the primary focus of attention; consumers are paying more attention to the design, packaging and brand of products. They are attracted by symbolic values such as taste, emotions and stories. The more affluent people become, the more attention they pay to emotive considerations behind their leisure, entertainment, cultural and health activities. Consumers are seeking out products that express their personal philosophy and social status. In today's society, consumption is no longer a means of satisfying basic needs. It has gradually become a kind of cultural declaration and a way of expressing a personalised sense of value. From a little backpack to a big family car, the cultural elements in consumer goods are influencing consumer choices. Therefore, combining cultural elements with traditional industries greatly increases the competitiveness of the latter. Creative design, thematic marketing and customized sales offers are ways to enhance the value added of cultural elements. Through consumption of products with traditional cultural elements, culture is made more productive and becomes a driving force in economic development.

Industrial Competitiveness

The simultaneous development of technological innovation and cultural creativity combines hard and soft approaches. Before analysing the contribution of creative industries to industrial competitiveness, we first need to look at the value system and the value creation process of creative industries.

From the perspective of consumers, the market value of a product consists of its use value and its symbolic value. Use value reflects what the consumer is willing to pay for the functional properties of the goods. It is the material basis of the goods, made possible by technology. Symbolic value refers to the intangible elements that respond to the emotional needs or cultural aspirations of social groups.

Adding value is satisfying customer demand; it is also about a shift from use value to symbolic value. When we invent a product, we initially put emphasis on use value. But when the product technology becomes commonplace, we need to apply different marketing and design strategies which put symbolic value at the core.

In 2005, W. Chan Kim and Renee Mauborgne from INSEAD published a business strategy book called *Blue Ocean Strategy*.[23] The book was an instant success and provoked a tremendous response globally. The Blue Ocean Strategy model illustrates the need to provide new value elements and to explore new markets. My understanding is that creative industries play an important role in this strategy by asking enterprises to turn their attention from supply to demand, away from attempting to beat their competitors and towards providing new symbolic elements for consumers. By adding such elements and eliminating old value elements, enterprises can hope to escape the bloody competition of the

---

[23] W. Chan Kim and Renee Mauborgne *Blue Ocean Strategy* (Cambridge: Harvard Business Press, 2005).

'red ocean' and open up a new market space in the 'blue ocean' where they can provide these new elements at relatively low cost.

The way to maximize value is to combine creative ideas, technology, the product and its market. Of these four the creative idea is the core element because it is responsible for the distribution of the value chain and the extension of value. Technology supports the communication and development of cultural creativity as well as the transfer of value. The product (including services) is the carrier of cultural meanings while the market is the exchange platform, the place where value is realized. From an industry perspective the key is to establish a value realization system, not simply to produce a product with the four elements combined.

The value system consists of four groups of industries, namely core, facilitating, supporting and spin-off industries. Each of these groups has its own supporting enterprises. At the core are enterprises that produce creative goods and services and that are responsible for value creation and extension of the value chain. The facilitating industries provide the key production inputs and services in the fields of science and technology, finance, media and advertising. The supporting industries in turn provide skill training and product promotion. Enterprises in this group include tourism, hospitality, entertainment and education and training. Spin-off industries produce outputs such as toys, stationery, fashion, accessories, bags and suitcases, food and souvenirs.

Market share is the most common index for assessing industrial competitiveness. China operates a deficit in cultural trade even though it has an overall trade surplus. In contrast, the success of the 'Korean Wave' shows that apart from effective organization of cultural production, South Korea has benefited from showcasing Eastern culture. China has rich resources in traditional culture which should be a huge advantage in increasing its competitiveness.

Soft Power

The concept of soft power was coined by Joseph Nye in 1990.[24] Nye believes the comprehensive strength of a country or a region includes not only the hard power of the economy, military strength and natural resources, but also

[24] Joseph Nye, 'Soft power' *Foreign Policy* 80: 1999, pp. 153–171; also Nye, *Power in the Global Information Age* (London: Routledge, 2004).

'soft power'. The soft power of a nation is made up of many kinds of power: political, diplomatic and cultural. But the core constituent is cultural, a country or region's established or shared philosophy, its values, and basic beliefs.

The report of the Chinese Communist Party's 17th National Party Congress in 2007 emphasized the importance attached to 'cultural soft power'. The report noted that culture is increasingly an important source of national cohesion and creativity and a key factor in overall national strength. The more attractive a country's image is, the stronger is its soft power.[25] While three decades of economic reform and opening up has witnessed marked progress, China's image has not improved to the same extent. China enjoys a growing international position; its international influence has expanded with a growing interest in Chinese studies across the world. Its cultural resources, however, are underutilized. Other nations have made profits out of tapping into China's cultural resources. Hollywood made *Mulan* and *Kung Fu Panda* while Japan has turned China's popular novels *Journey to the West* and *Romans of Three Kingdoms* into animations and video games. Creativity is a new strategic choice for China; first, to utilize existing cultural resources with modern elements; secondly, to combine creativity, technology and market demand to develop high-value-added cultural and creative industries while opening international markets for culture-rich products and services.

[25] http://news.xinhuanet.com/newscenter/2007-10/24/content_6938568.htm [accessed 8 March 2011].

2

The Transformation of China's Economy

The Issue

The past thirty years of reform and opening up have produced tremendous changes in China. China's economy has grown so fast and maintained growth for so long that this is generally considered an economic 'miracle.' But behind such rapid growth, problems have arisen that are not conducive to sustainable social development. China's growth is achieved at the expense of the environment and natural resources. A priority issue is how to transform this growth model into a creative economy model. Whereas the growth model is driven by investment and at the expense of resources, the creative economy model is driven by consumption. In the latter model, creativity and innovation are the investments.

The international financial crisis which started in 2008 sank the global economy into recession. China's economy slowed as many export-oriented and investment-driven industries were affected. Export trade in the first three months of 2009 was down 24 per cent from the previous year confirming a downward trend in the economy. International cities such as Beijing and Shanghai faced problems of weakened industries, increased business costs and a worsening urban ecology. At the same time, it became apparent that the industrial heritage of receding manufacturing industries was providing development space for economic transformation.

In this chapter I address the following questions: First, how might traditional industries increase value added and maintain competitiveness? Second, how should resource-reliant manufacturing industries adjust their industrial structures? Third, how might creative industries invest in related industries in order to leverage coordinated economic development?

I have discussed such issues in my earlier book *Study on the Transformation of Economic Growth Models*.[1] I was one of the first economists to propose a link

---

[1] Wuwei Li and Huiming Wang, *Study on the Transformation of Economic Growth Models* (Shanghai: Hok-lam Press, 2006).

between creative industries and the transformation of economic development models. As early as 2005, I initiated the idea that creative industries are an industrial form that adapts to the knowledge economy. I argued that cultural creativity and technological innovation are the two driving engines for increasing industry value added and competitiveness. In terms of industrial structure, creative industries are characterized by the application of high technology; creativity permeates industrial production processes ranging from primary to service industries. At the heart of creative industries is innovation, which is why many developed countries, after achieving industrialization, have recognized innovation to be an important strategic initiative to stimulate economic transformation and competitiveness.

China is at a critical point in its development. The global economic crisis, caused by the financial crisis, has quickened the pace at which China is upgrading and adapting its industrial structure. China's central cities, now in a post-industrial era, are facing substantive challenges, including the depletion of natural resources, increasing pressure on the environment, the decline of manufacturing industries and the impact of these things on quality of life. To maintain a sustainable economy, China needs to bring about a fundamental transformation of its economic model. In other words, China needs to change the current investment-driven, economic growth model characterized by high consumption of resources, high pollution, excessive production capacity and low value added. China should actively seek a new economic form, in which the industrial structure will be rational, the economy can develop in an orderly way and socially sustainable development can be achieved. The creative economy is just such an economic form.

Creative Industries in the Economic Crisis

During 2008 and 2009 when the Chinese economy was affected by the global economic recession, the creative industries experienced breakthrough growth. In 2008, China's online games sector achieved sales income of RMB 18.38 billion, up 76.6 per cent from the previous year, as well as export growth of over 20 per cent. The animation industry achieved a growth of over 46 per cent. The total revenue from radio, film and television (including financial assistance income) in 2008 was up by 20.49 per cent from the previous year.[2] Box office takings increased by 35 per cent; in January and February 2009 the box office was 110 per cent up from the same period in 2008. In 2009, stimulated by a series of central government policies to 'maintain capital growth, expand domestic demand and readjust structure', GDP growth reached 8.7 per cent. The creative industries moreover achieved an overall growth of 17 per cent, making an important contribution to the Chinese economy.[3]

In recent years, the growth of creative industries in many regions of China has been higher than the conventional economic growth indicators. In 2007, general GDP growth in Beijing, Shanghai and Shenzhen was 12.3 per cent, 13.3 per cent and 15 per cent respectively while that of creative industries in those cities was 19.4 per cent, 22.8 per cent and 25.9 per cent. In the second-tier cities it has been a similar story. In 2008, for instance, value added by creative industries in Hangzhou and Qingdao reached RMB 57.986 billion and RMB 31.9 billion respectively, up by 17.6 per cent and 22.6 per cent. Creative industries in China's middle and western areas have performed well. The value added of creative industries in 2008 in Chongqing, for instance, reached RMB 24 billion while Changsha had RMB 27 billion, an annual growth of 30 per cent and 17 per cent respectively.[4]

International experience shows that creative industries have played a key role in times of economic crisis and in turn have stimulated the development of new industries. Hollywood and Disney rose out of the Great Depression of the 1930s; Japan's animation success emerged from the oil crisis of the 1970s; IT and content industries sprang up during the 1997 Asian financial crisis and reversed the economic downslide. Japan and South Korea had similar experiences. During the Asian financial crisis, South Korea suffered economic depression and a sharp increase in unemployment. People who lost their jobs killed time and released frustration by spending many hours playing internet games. The government seized this opportunity to encourage the development of animation and gaming, thus generating momentum in these sectors. Taking advantage of this impetus

[2] According to the 2009 Blue Book of Radio and Television (*Development Report of China's Radio and Television 2009*), (Beijing: Xinhua Press, 2009).

[3] 2009–2010 China Cultural Creative Industries Development Research Report. CCID Consulting, China http://www.docin.com/p-67596359.html [accessed 8 March 2011].

[4] Jingcheng Zhang, *Chinese Creative Industries Report (2009)*, (Beijing: China Economic Publishing House, 2009).

and fully supported by government, South Korea's film and television industries, together with the music industry, took off. A 'Korean wave' ensued across Asia, assisting tourism and the export of South Korean products. It was the development of creative industries that helped the country's recovery from the financial crisis. Again, during the 2008 world financial crisis, Japanese *manga* saw a big growth in trade while at the same time undertaking the social role of assuring public confidence.[5] These cases show that it is the outpouring and accumulation of creative power that have helped nations in times of economic crisis.

An interesting phenomenon in economics is referred to as the 'lipstick effect'. In the US it has been observed that whenever the economy is not in good shape, sales of lipsticks rise. Why is this? When the economy is not good income and consumption habits are affected. Anxiety about the future is expressed in degrees of psychological stress that need to be relieved. The demand-oriented creative industries have seen this as an opportunity and have taken to providing a 'happy world' in which the public can release stress and frustration. In times of economic crisis, people tend to buy less expensive luxuries. Hence lipstick, as something 'cheap and non-essential', becomes female consumers' preferred choice. The same can be said about consumption of cultural products. When there is more leisure time but an inverse proportion of income, people tend to seek psychological comfort through consuming cheap goods. They like to go to movies, play games and watch animated cartoons to obtain a sense of satisfaction at a reasonable price. At the same time society needs creative industries to provide cultural expressions that help restore the public's confidence in the future. US movies have benefitted in the past from the 'lipstick effect'. The Great Depression of the 1920s and 1930s gave birth to the cartoon image of Mickey Mouse, the musical *The Wizard of Oz*, the classic film *Gone with the Wind*, the comedy of Charlie Chaplin and many film production companies.

Creativity and Innovation

For China the significance of creative industries is not limited to a new 'industry' concept; nor is it confined to the production and export of cultural

---

[5] Xiaoxu Wang (2009), 'Financial Crisis is the Opportunity to Boost The Culture Industry,' *Hubei Daily*, 2 June 2009.

and creative products. Rather, the significance lies in a capacity to stimulate innovation in established industries and bring about systemic innovation more broadly. Industrial innovation has become an urgent and important project. Currently, China's reliance on foreign technology is over 50 per cent. 70 per cent of new technologies come from foreign sources.[6] With increasing pressure on resources and the environment, China's manufacturing industries must increase their innovation capacity in order to change the production mode of low value added, high resource consumption and high levels of pollution.

China needs innovative spirit. John Howkins believes the biggest problem China faces is how to transform from a manufacturing country with cost as its main source of competitiveness into a creative economy with innovation as its main competitive advantage. Creative industries go beyond the scope of traditional cultural industries, regrouping human and cultural capital and bringing it into the economic system. By utilizing creativity, for instance, established industries can add more cultural elements to products and services and bring about differentiated competition. They can also build distinctive brands so as to increase competitiveness. Cultural creativity can be incorporated into the design of all kinds of products and even into urban construction. The use of colour to cater to people's mood, the use of design to provide physical comforts and operational convenience, and the design of unique shapes and features serve to effectively increase the value added of products.

Intellectual Property (IP)

Apart from encouraging innovation and high value added, intellectual property protection is a means of expanding creative industries and strengthening the commercialization of innovation. IP is at the core of creative industries' value chain. This idea has been largely accepted across the world. Creativity can create wealth if it takes place through the development and utilization of intellectual property. The process is cultural creativity → intellectual property → wealth creation. Due to the fact that creative products normally have more visible external expressions

---

[6] Wuwei Li (2009), 'Proposal on including Creative Industries in the National Innovation Plan,' *Economic Daily*, 21 May 2009. http://www.chinanews.com.cn/cj/cj-cyzh/news/2009/05-21/1701840.shtml [accessed 8 March 2011].

than new scientific products, they are more likely to be copied and plagiarized. Therefore creative industries are in greater need of IP protection.

China has already produced a series of IP-related legislation such as patent law, copyright law, trademark law and laws corresponding to their implementation. A legal framework has developed regarding IP in compliance with international law. From a micro perspective, an enterprise IP strategy should be implemented that includes the creation, trade and management of intellectual property. For creative enterprises, IP is their most important asset as cultural and creative results can only be turned into industrial products and achieve maximum profits through the creation and commercial operation of intellectual property. The creation of intellectual property includes attaining patent or copyright through technological innovation and cultural creativity, and by extension building brands and registering trademarks. In other words, enterprises should not only acquire and retain core intellectual property (copyright for a cultural and creative result) but also obtain as much related external intellectual property as possible. This will constitute a powerful IP safety net and ensure the maximization of economic benefits.

A good example is the web song *Mouse Loves Rice* which has not only obtained copyright but also been registered as a trademark. The song has become a brand.[7] Through IP, it has gained earnings from concerts, release of discs, karaoke and ringtones. Through branding, it has been developed into a novel, a musical movie, a TV drama series and a suite of mobile games, all carrying the same name. This example demonstrates that patent, copyright, brand and trademark can be commercial operation tools. Disney's success is based on a similar process: creating a story, producing an animation concept, attracting audiences, registering a brand, making related products, and reaping huge profits. The animated characters they have developed such as Mickey Mouse, Donald Duck, and The Lion King have generated considerable wealth from IP.

Creative industries are characterized by large numbers of small and medium-sized enterprises (SMEs). These companies are weak in terms of protecting their rights and it is not feasible for the government to take direct responsibility for such a large number and range of SMEs. So SMEs need to cooperate and help each other in legal matters. In April 2004, twenty-three enterprises at Tianzifang, a creative

[7] The song 'Mouse loves Rice' was composed by Chengang Yang. http://yule.sohu.com/20050513/n225548156.shtml [accessed 8 March 2011].

industries cluster in Shanghai, established the Tianzifang IP Protection Alliance to pool resources for IP protection, industry self-regulation and collaborative marketing. Based on this experience and supported by the municipal government's IP bureau, a city-wide IP protection alliance was established in May 2008 with improved and expanded services. Protected by this alliance, market competitiveness of a large number of SMEs in Shanghai has been markedly improved.

Risks and Benefits

Creative industries are characterized by high risk and high benefits. The value of cultural and creative companies is determined by products and by human capital assets. Many factors can affect the IP value of cultural products, which results in uncertainty in business activities.

What kinds of risks are involved in creative business activities? What are the types and features of these risks?

Creative products are uncertain in terms of demand

The demand for cultural and creative products is different from that of industrial products (or the products of material industries) such as electric rice cookers. It is relatively easy to predict the demand for such things. The demand for cultural and creative products is difficult to predict as there is no utility demand for these kinds of products. Consequently, there is uncertainty in demand. For instance, it is hard to predict audiences for a movie because consumer choice can be affected by a number of factors such as the theme of the movie, the nature of the marketing, the income level of the audience, the nature of distribution and the extent of word-of-mouth promotion. This is why it is normal practice for the film industry to predict box office success based on past experiences. Although *Avatar* was predicted to bring in a total income of US$ one billion for investors, it was only after the film had premiered that the actual demand for it became evident.

Creativity is easy to copy

A good idea is not easy to come up with. Dissemination of the idea, however, costs almost nothing. For example, it is hard to turn out a good idea for a movie; but the resulting script can be easily copied and disseminated by other people. Without sound IP protection, creative ideas are likely to be copied. The end result could be that copycats benefit from other people's work without being punished while the creators won't get due returns for their high-risk investment.

Cultural products do not have physical forms

Unlike products that have their own physical forms and are difficult to copy and disseminate, such as housing and electric rice cookers, cultural products and services (such as design, film and TV products and game software) are often digital artefacts and a easy prey for copycats. For instance, the cost of reproducing a DVD of a movie, a TV series or music is low and the production process is easy. This is the technological reason for frequent pirating. IP protection is therefore very important. It cost US$300 million to make *Avatar*, but the cost of making a DVD copy is almost nothing.

There is uncertainty in technology, process and market acceptance

The production of creative products (the realization of creativity) may require technology; the production process may take a long time; and the final product may or may not be accepted by the market. This is another risk for creative products. Film is a good example by way of illustration: the production process involves a lengthy chain; the producers often have no control over the distribution and screening processes. This adds to uncertainty in the film industry.

This was the case with *Avatar*. To achieve the extraordinary 3D visual effects, the production costs reached US$300 million and it took twelve years and the production of numerous computer special effects. The process involved not only artistic creativity and high production costs but also the development and application of new technology.

Not all big investments can expect high returns. Huge investment in culture and creativity may result in low or even no returns. With a box office income of 1.35 billion yuan on the Chinese market, *Avatar* is a rare exception. Generally speaking, at least 60 per cent of film investment loses money. Of the 400–500 movies produced annually on the Chinese film market, only 100 to 120 movies are screened in cinema chains. Among these, 30 per cent makes money, 40 per cent break even and 30 per cent lose money. It is similar story in other film markets across the world.

The phenomenon of *shanzhai*

Innovation and imitation are two sides of the same coin: they exist alongside China's great leap forward from backwards technology to advanced research and development, with China's transformation from large-scale imitation to originality. *Shanzhai* (cheap copy, copycat) is a word that has been popular in China since 2008. It first appeared in the IT industry in 2005 when a large number of small factories flourished in Shenzhen, Zhejiang and Jiangsu, engaged in producing cheap copies of famous brands including mobile phones and digital products. Some made modifications to the famous brands, turning Nokia to Nokir, Samsung to Samsing and Sony-Ericsson to Suny-Ericcsun. Though there is some innovation involved in the production process, in copying authentic products these factories do not need to spend money on R&D; so they are able to sell these products at a much lower price, at one-fifth of the cost of the authentic products and sometimes even less. As a result, there is considerable impact on the market. This kind of copycat activity later spread to cultural formats and products such as paintings, and movies. Even the Spring Festival Evening Party, an annual event celebrating Chinese New Year broadcast on the national network, China Central TV, was not spared the *shanzhai* treatment. *Shanzhai* has since become a synonym for 'imitation,' 'copycat' and 'fake.'

An article published on *Lianhe zaobao*[8] in Singapore suggests that *shanzhai* is a phenomenon in which mainstream brands are copied at low cost and innovated in terms of product functions. '*Shanzhai* culture' therefore refers to a highly mediated or highly disputed cultural phenomenon in which existing products (including cultural products) are redesigned, reproduced and marketed, usually at a cheaper price. Rather than generalizing the *shanzhai* phenomenon in the negative sense, we should differentiate good and bad *shanzhai* products, *shanzhai* cultures and *shanzhai* economies on a case-by-case basis.

First, *shanzhai* products are an example of copying, violation of rights and pirating. They represent an illegal act and violation of intellectual property rights. The act should be punished by administrative means or even taken to court.

[8] Yongxin Yang (2009), 'Do not enjoy the short-term pleasure of copy-cat', *Lianhe Zaobao*, Singapore. 5 Mar 2009. http://www.chinanews.com.cn/hb/news/2009/03-05/1589554.shtml

Although the superficial functions of *shanzhai* products may contain a certain degree of innovation and originality, *shanzhai* production is motivated by the pursuit of low-cost operation, tax evasion and short-term economic benefits. The *shanzhai* phenomenon reflects a series of social problems including a lack of effective supply in low-end market segments, the unwillingness of some enterprises to invest in R&D, the lack of IP protection, and weakness in policy and supervision of regulations. The establishment and implementation of an IP protection system has become one of the major challenges for China's transition to an innovative nation.

Second, the 'shanzhai culture' or the low-cost copying of cultural products is in fact a kind of popular culture that is non-mainstream, anti-elite and challenges authority. It is a 'grassroots' culture with postmodern, deconstructive characteristics. It is often an act of popular culture in which people give full rein to their imagination and creativity for the purposes of self-entertainment. It is not always for profit and is often disseminated on networks that are outside the control of mainstream media. In contrast to authentic mainstream productions which are often costly and unpopular, *shanzhai* versions employ sarcasm, humour and grassroots language; in doing so they engage people's emotions. Through this practice, the grassroots creators challenge the mainstream with the marginal, the professional with the amateur.

When cultural production and mass communication are dominated by mainstream cultural institutions, many people try to enjoy cultural autonomy through this unique mode of imitation. In a way, *shanzhai* culture signifies the awakening of civic consciousness. It is a social phenomenon of self expression and creative expression. In this sense, society should be more tolerant of its existence as long as it is not conducted for economic benefit alone. Such tolerance would allow more space for people's cultural creativity and would be of benefit in terms of cultural competition and the development of cultural diversity.

Third, the *shanzhai* economy, a model of production by imitation, can be harmful for economic development and the process of modernization. Sociologist Ai Jun believes that the 'shanzhai model' is inevitable in developing countries. However, he says the economy should move beyond the 'shanzhai model' as soon as possible. Other economists agree that developing countries have the opportunity to take advantage as latecomers to catch up with advanced countries, particularly through the introduction of advanced technologies.

It is undeniable that one of the reasons for the rapid development of the Chinese economy in the past thirty years is the formation of global competitive advantages in manufacturing industries through the introduction of foreign capital and technology, technological transformation, cheap labour and the consumption of natural resources. Economic growth has been achieved largely through exports. I argue, however, that a nation that relies solely on imitation and lacks innovation has no future. The *shanzhai* economy is an unsustainable economic development model. *Shanzhai* products may bring short-term economic benefits for enterprises and consumers, but over time who would want to invest in R&D and originality if the interests of innovators and intellectual property cannot be effectively protected?

If a general mindset for imitation and opportunism is allowed to develop, the ability to innovate and create intellectual property will be limited to a few developed countries or advanced enterprises. The danger of the loss of innovative ability is real. China's small and medium-sized enterprises should encourage entrepreneurs to recognize innovation, risk-taking, risk management and risk commitment. Alternatively, government and regulators need to take necessary measures to contain *shanzhai* practice by fighting against piracy, by protecting intellectual property and by regulating the environment in which business operates.

Innovative Nation

For over half a century countries around the world have been looking for ways to realize industrialization and modernization from their respective points of departure. The international academic community defines an innovative nation as one that undertakes technological innovation as its basic economic strategy. Currently there are around twenty recognized innovative nations, including the United States, Japan, Finland and South Korea. Their common features are a high innovation index, over 70 per cent contribution of technological progress to economic growth, R&D investment accounting for over 2 per cent of GDP and lower than 30 per cent reliance on foreign technology.[9]

At the 2006 National Conference of Science and Technology in Beijing Chinese President Hu Jintao announced China's intention to become an

[9] Innovation Country: http://baike.baidu.com/view/58084.htm [accessed 8 March 2011].

innovative nation by 2020. The basic indicator for this is the contribution of scientific technology and innovation to economic growth, which will have to increase from 39 per cent to 60 per cent and the ratio of R&D investment in GDP which will have to increase from 1.35 per cent to 2.5 per cent. The latest results from the *Study on Scientific Contribution to Economic Development*, a national science research project, show that from 1980 to 2007 the total factor productivity (TFP) contribution to economic growth was 45.62 per cent and the rate of technological progress was 4.53 per cent. The research predicts that by 2020 scientific contribution may reach around 60 per cent. Increasing innovative capacity is becoming the central link in China's effort to readjust its economic structure, transform its development model and increase national competitiveness.

The Way to Economic Growth

Economic statistics indicate that the Chinese economy is recovering. However, the fundamental problems (or the contradictions caused by the imbalance of internal and external economic structures) that led to the economic downturn are yet to be solved. New consumer markets need to be opened and new hot spots of demand need to be created. During the transformation period, changing the approach to economic development will enable the Chinese economy to gain new momentum. To solve the problem of structural imbalance and to create a new growth engine, we need to transform and upgrade the economy. Creative industries will stimulate the transformation of the Chinese economy from the export-oriented approach to innovation-driven approach.

From the perspective of industry development, there are two ways to stimulate the transformation of China's economic growth. One is to increase the value added of China's manufacturing industries through upgrading, readjusting and innovating in terms of industrial structures. The other way is to develop new, innovative, eco-friendly industries with growth potential. Creative industries will help the Chinese economy to recover from the financial crisis and to open new markets.

Shenzhen, the frontier city of China's reform and opening up, has seized the opportunity to stimulate transformation through cultural and creative industries. For its achievements in December of 2008 Shenzhen was named 'City of Design' by UNESCO. UNESCO also approved Shenzhen's application to join the UNESCO creative cities network. Shenzhen's approach is to combine branding with product design in an effort to drive transformation: to move from selling products to selling designs, from a focus on manufacturing industries to a focus on design industries; in other words, from a processing centre to a city of design. Taking advantage of its status as global 'City of Design', Shenzhen attracts international creative resources (including design talent, international exhibitions and creative enterprises) and promotes its design across China and across the world. The cultural expo held in Shenzhen in April 2009 attracted 3.5 million visitors (1.65 million more than the previous year) and achieved a business turnover of RMB 87.7 billion (RMB 37.8 billion more than the previous year). Currently, Shenzhen has 60 per cent of market share in the domestic industrial design market.[10] Design reflects a higher position than some manufacturing and processing industries in the value chain. In the face of a financial crisis and the loss of policy advantages once held by processing and manufacturing industries, creative industries, and especially the design industry are expected to become a new advantage for Shenzhen.

Creative industries can also play a key role in the second approach to China's economic growth transformation, namely the promoting of new industries. Many creative industries are emerging industries that have come into being as the world has shifted to a knowledge economy. In the next few years, the combination of culture and technology will give rise to new industrial forms and communication channels. The boundaries between industries will become increasingly blurred. With technological innovation and large-scale development, cable TV network and wireless mobile networks are becoming important platforms for the integration of cultural and creative resources. Online libraries and newspapers, IPTV, digital cinema, video-on-demand, and TV and film content formatted for mobile devices are blurring industry boundaries even more. Digital technology is entering into a high-speed, large-scale commercial phase with unlimited market potential.

[10] Fang Ni, (2010), 'The 4th Emerging Strategic Industry: Shenzhen's Creative Industries on the Road,' *Nanfang Daily*, 10 Aug 2010. Available at http://www.ceosz.cn/SzNews/SzYw/SzNews_20100811104908_55445_5.html [accessed 8 March 2011].

Emerging industries should be understood beyond their role in the sphere of industry. They should be understood in terms of their role in overturning and bringing about innovations in traditional economic development models, in upgrading industry structures, and in increasing overall regional competitiveness. To develop emerging industries so as to stimulate a new round of economic growth for China, we need to change the old strategy of following in the footsteps of others and replace the 'advantage of the latecomer' with a strategy driven by innovation.

Industries without Boundaries

In traditional economic theories of industry, an industry refers to a collective of enterprises that provides similar products and services. This implies artificially imposed boundaries between industries. In the twenty-first century, one characterized by a focus on markets, information and internationalization, however, the development models of conventional industries have experienced profound change. New approaches have led to expanded scale and scope of economic development, accelerated cycles of development, structural upgrading and greater systemic complexity. It has become inevitable for industry development to proceed from division of labour toward integration. These developments cannot be explained by traditional theories that worked well when industries had clear boundaries. For instance, new forms of industry such as cultural and information industries hardly belong to any of the old industry categories. We need to change our development concepts from being defined by division of labour so as to adapt to these new circumstances.

Creative industries are industries 'without boundaries'.[11] Industries without boundaries have three features:

- Integration with related industries: industries without boundaries can be integrated into related industries and continuously regenerate through technology. It is very difficult to define the boundaries between the industries or to place then within the traditional categories of industry;

---

[11] Apart from making it possible to re-categorize the industries involved, the significance of this concept lies in in creative industries' impact on the evolution of industry structures.

- Soft elements as core competitiveness: in contrast to traditional industries which have increasing marginal cost and diminishing marginal revenue, industries without boundaries are characterized by diminishing marginal costs and increasing marginal revenue;

- Constant changes of boundaries: industries without boundaries are directly driven by consumption. Their resources, key industrial elements and operations are constantly reorganized according to constantly changing demand. The diverse and changing nature of demand contributes to the uncertainty of boundaries.

Why are creative industries 'industries without boundaries'?

First, innovations can be integrated with established cultural industries. A typical example is the online bookstore which has become an important channel for book consumption, providing instant information about new books and a personalized interface for consumers. In saving time and simplifying purchase procedures, online bookstores are reducing costs and providing more benefits to the reader. However, the online bookstore cannot provide the reader with the sensation and joy of roaming between bookshelves and flipping through the pages of new books. The reader can only find this in traditional bookstores. So there is a mutually supportive interaction between online and traditional bookstores, in which the boundaries between online and offline, virtual and physical are blurred. There is an element of reality in the virtual and an element of the virtual in physical reality. This kind of integration is stimulating the book sales industry.

Second, the extensive use of information technology together with a fundamental change in the mode of production have broken the traditional boundaries between the various cultural sectors and have led to more cross-penetration and integration. The customary idea of 'competition with clearly defined boundaries' among manufacturers has been replaced by an intersecting, and broader concept. In the process of coordinating related activities, there is cooperation as well as competition. Based on integrated digital technology, for example, there is increasing business integration among services, content and applications. Newspapers, TV, music, magazines, sport and other forms of entertainment have adopted online mixed multimedia formats. Such integration has broken through the division of labour restrictions and has enabled telecommunications, media and information technology enterprises to establish cross products, cross platforms and revenue-sharing across sectors. This in turn has led to rational allocation of resources on a larger scale while bringing big business opportunities for enterprises.

Third, creative industries can achieve integration across boundaries. The principal components of creative industries are creative products; for instance in design industries this might include the idea for the design, a theme, a project plan, and ways of producing and marketing these. But creative industries often generate value through related products. Positioned in the upstream of the industry value chain, creative industries are able to achieve boundary-less integration. The significance is not limited to the pursuit of productivity in culture itself. The significance also lies in the production and application of creative achievements in various trades, industries and fields. This is an effective way to improve capacity and value added of industries.

Lastly, creative industries can achieve diffusion across boundaries. In the knowledge economy the essence of product competition is to influence or cater to the values, habits and customs of the public through cultural elements represented in a product. The aim is to have the public accept the product. To be specific, cultural connotations, cultural value added and cultural uniqueness increase the competitiveness of a product. These include concept, design, modelling, style, decoration, packaging, trademark and advertising. Whether or not a product will be accepted by the consumer largely depends on the cultural identity of the product. Behind each of the popular products of the 'Korean Wave', the 'Hong Kong and Taiwan Style' and the 'European Style', there is a degree of cultural accumulation in play. The significance of an excellent product goes beyond the product itself. The cultural element in the product has turned the consumption of the product into the consumption of culture. The in-built capacity of culture to diffuse enhances the product's marketability. The charm of creative industries is their capacity to diffuse across boundaries.

Transformation of Economic Development Mode

Resources transformation, value upgrade, structural optimization and market expansion are four models for the transformation of the existing model for economic development in China.

Resources transformation

As a result of the current model of extensive economic development huge quantities of material resources, especially energy, are becoming exhausted. Economic growth is at the cost of natural resources and the environment. Constraints on resources, environment and capital have become a bottleneck to economic development. Creative industries, however, are characterized by the continual release of individual creativity, generating new products and market demand by breaking through the constraints on resources.[12] This model can be understood from the following three perspectives:

First, when creativity becomes a leading resource in economic growth, the definition of resources is expanded. More elements can be included in the definition of 'resources', such as historical artefacts, folklore and elements of social life. These elements can be exploited and developed to promote economic growth.

Second, through developing humankind's intellectual capacity, that is, creativity, various resources – natural and cultural, tangible and intangible – can be effectively transformed into capital for economic development. For instance, a neglected river corridor in Chengdu, Sichuan Province provides a good example. The local government did not have the money to support the Jinjiang River redevelopment project and so decided to involve investors. Through market research and planning, a 6,000 square metre raised level was added as a commercial venue and the river corridor was restored. The restaurant on the upper level now has the best river view of the area, attracting swarms of customers. This is a win–win deal for the local government and the investors. This is also a good example of effective use of resources.

Third, the 'human brain' is a resource that can be exploited to 'make something out of nothing' and 'produce excellence out of something'. Creativity can break through the constraints of finite resources and promote economic growth; it can stimulate transformations among various kinds of capital (economic, cultural and social). This in turn means economic development relies more on cultural and social capital (the soft elements) as its driving force. This soft infrastructure model is characterized by a combination of

---

[12] Through creativity various resources can be turned into capital, which opens up new channels and markets for economic development. This model, when put into practice, will generate a process of multiple transformations from resources to capital and beyond to the market. These transformations will in turn promote the transformation of the model of economic growth.

creativity and technology, of creativity and markets. In its almost 100 years of development, Disney has continuously increased innovation and technology in its products according to market demand and in so doing has become a global entertainment brand. Its range of products, such as animation, toys, clothes, home décor and theme parks have not only made huge profits but have introduced a new development model for the entertainment industries. Britain's *Harry Potter* series is a typical example of 'producing excellence out of something'. The production of literature is an age-old profession. But *Harry Potter* has turned its author, J.K. Rowling from a poor teacher into a very rich person whose wealth rivals that of the Queen. It is a contemporary legend of wealth creation. The key to *Harry Potter*'s success is a combination of technology and the market; similarly many related products are produced to meet different levels of demand, ranging from hi-tech digital products such as movies, DVDs and games, to everyday items such as toys and clothes. Between related and derivative products industrial chains are established. Crude statistics show that related industries driven by *Harry Potter* have achieved a total economic turnover of US$200 billion.[13]

Value upgrade

As mentioned in chapter one, we can divide the market value of goods into use value and symbolic value. The former represents the objective functions of the product (its usefulness) while the latter refers to the subjective intangibles that appeal to the human senses. The use value is enabled by technology and is the material basis of a product. The symbolic conceptual value refers to the cultural values embedded in the product. The ratio of the two components will change with economic development. In times marked by low-level economic development, outdated technology and material shortage, people pay attention to the utility of a product. But when the economy is doing better and people are well-off they may be more attracted to symbolic values. The market value of a product is increasingly determined by its symbolic value.[14] In a general sense,

[13] http://www.dushu.com/news/2007/08-31/19979.html [accessed 8 March 2011].
[14] When we are in the age of knowledge economy where the exchange and expansion of technology is stepped up and commodities are in rich supply and tend to homogenize, the ratio of the concept value will be higher and people are more likely to identify with the intangibles in the product or services, such as class, feelings, sensations, appeals and meaning.

the symbolic value creates distinctiveness, contributing value added over and above the product quality. The essence of creativity is to produce satisfaction and happiness through exploitation of the symbolic value, to maximize the product's effectiveness and make the consumer feel happy.

Structural optimization

Creative industries demonstrate the integrated development of culture, science and economy. This kind of integration is established on the basis of providing highly personalized creative products for the consumer. This requires, on the one hand, diversified cultural resources and markets for cultural expansion. In addition, this also heavily relies on information technology. Only in virtual space can a personalized environment be created in which 'there is nothing you cannot achieve except that which you had not thought of'. Cultural elements and technological capability are important factors contributing to optimizing the existing economic development structure.

Every creative activity is carried out against a certain cultural background. Culture is the core element in creative industries' attempt to promote the transformation of the economic growth mode. Culture can bring about immeasurable value added.[15] Creative industries use culture as a 'sharp instrument' to cut through a path for new industry models. The application of digital technology has enabled creative industries to integrate with a variety of other industries and trades.

The optimization of industrial structure comes in two modes. The first is structural optimization of traditional cultural resources, which are recreated and upgraded with wisdom, inspiration and imagination. The second mode is the structural optimization of existing industries. Industrial design, branding and marketing in creative industries have not only increased value added of manufacturing industries but have also enabled more flexible industrial structures. In urban agriculture, integration with tourism has brought about big changes. New features such as sightseeing, tourism and ecology are reaping profits. For instance, ticket sales at the Shanghai Port of Fresh Flowers have surpassed the actual sales of flowers. Currently, the Yangzi River Delta area has adopted agricultural tourism as a new approach to structurally benefit

---

[15] See Li Wuwei, 2004. Culture can 'graft' seamlessly onto other industries; its links and products can subsequently form new industry sectors.

agriculture. Agricultural tourism has transformed from a model largely based on small scale cultivation and sporadic business. The integration of tourism represents a new regional mode of regional development.

Market expansion

The use of the cultural capacity of brands to identify with and form enduring relationships with consumers has become a highly intensive knowledge-based form of market competition. The construction of a brand must first identify the core competitiveness or the core value that differentiates the brand from others. The core value is the idea while at the heart of a brand is the producer's ability to identify and align his creative work and his own understanding of the world with the target market. There are four approaches by which creativity promotes brand construction and market expansion through advertising.

The first approach is by developing products that reinterpret national classics. Culture can be exhibited and maintained in traditional and modern forms in film, music, multimedia, drama and on the internet. A good example is *The Dream of Red Mansions*, a much loved Chinese classic novel from the Qing Dynasty. This classic has not depreciated with time. On the contrary, new value has been continuously generated from it. Value has been created from the original classic novel to forms of opera, comics, ballet and recordings before the 1980s, to TV drama, film, multimedia, CDs and karaoke since the 1990s, and more recently to entertainment shows, animation, SMS and web games.

A second approach is to develop local resources for the global market. In today's era of economic globalization, many products tend to be thematically similar, as well as similar in content and style. The globalization of cultural products is inevitable and has led to homogenization of aesthetic standards. On the one hand, brand expansion strategies pay attention to cultural trends in order to adapt to the global market demand. This strategy develops unique resources by repackaging historical figures, folk legends, science education and everyday themes.

A third approach is to innovate in development, that is, to establish an unprecedented, new, modern cultural and creative brand. Creative ideas are crucial to the success of a brand. They are dreams based on reality. A cultural and creative brand is a creation completely made by the producer, or the content value created by the creative entrepreneur. It can normally fit comfortably with modern views of consumption.

Last but not least, advertising greatly impacts the building of creative brands by establishing positive associations between the brand and the consumers. Advertising helps creative brands establish a good industry image and in turn promotes brand development. In a market economy advertising is one of the leading creative industries. The development of advertising directly expands markets. To a certain extent, we can say that without the support of advertising, the existing business approach of the media industries cannot survive.

Policy Suggestions

I am pleased to see the development of creative industries in China. In 2004–2005 when I first proposed the concept of 'industries without boundaries' there was uproar in the academic and industrial communities. At that time, creative industries were still at the embryonic stage and most people did not have a clear idea of what they represented, the features of the industries and the development approach. After five years of exploration and practice, there is now consensus among government, industry and academia. In practice, we note a search for common ground, as well as a process of exploring and innovating according to local conditions.

After years of theoretical research and practical investigation I have come to realize that it is not enough for the development of creative industries to rely solely on a city's own ideas and strategies. Policy support from the central government is badly needed. So, at the two national congresses of 2008, I proposed the development idea of 'creative agriculture.' At the Second Session of the CPPCC National Committee in 2009, I delivered, on behalf of the KMT Central Committee, a speech entitled 'To develop the creative industries and to promote economic innovation and upgrading of traditional industries'. In this speech, I called again for the central government to make creative industries policies. I put forward the following three suggestions that have raised awareness from all sectors concerned:

- Creative industries should be accepted into the national innovation plan: because technological innovation and cultural creativity are the two driving engines of sustainable economic development, creative industries should be incorporated as an important part of the innovation plan.

- A national association of creative industries should be established as soon as possible: The aim of this will be to integrate various social forces to assist the government in promoting creative industries. This will help overcome the drawbacks of fragmentation and help carry out international exchange in a more extensive way.

- Policies promoting the development of creative industries should be implemented: This includes mechanisms to stimulate investment and financing and to ensure risk-sharing as well as policies of IP protection and operation and training of talent related to creative industries.

With wide support from the public the proposal attracted the attention of the CPC Central Committee and the State Council. The goal of 'actively developing creative industries' appeared for the first time in the central government's work report. On July 22, 2009, the executive meeting of the State Council chaired by Premier Wen Jiabao discussed and approved the 'Revitalization Plan for the Cultural Industries,' the first item of which is to step up the development of key cultural industries including cultural creativity, film and TV production, publishing and distribution, printing and manufacturing, advertising, performing arts and entertainment, cultural exhibition, digital content and animation. Another agenda item was to actively develop new forms of culture to stimulate cultural industries. The new industry forms include mobile multimedia broadcasting, web broadcasting and film, and mobile broadcasting and TV. There is no doubt that national policies on cultural and creative industries will provide strong policy support for nation-wide development of creative industries.

3

Changing Development Concepts

Thirty years ago Deng Xiaoping embarked on the reform, opening up and modernization of China. Deng's reforms triggered tremendous social and economic transformation. Domestically and internationally, technology is increasing China's competitiveness. Culture is also playing a leading role. In other words a coordinated development strategy involves 'innovation' and 'creativity.' If science and technology are considered 'hard power,' then cultural creativity might be regarded as 'soft power.'

The internet is a technological platform that facilitates communication and exchange: for instance, commodities and activities are able to reach markets without being constrained by time and space. This bears special significance for small creative businesses in China. 'Alibaba.com' created a miracle of e-commerce in China. Apart from the successful business model initiated by founder Ma Yun, Alibaba's core system is network technology. Similarly, the rise of Shanda Interactive Entertainment Ltd, a leading interactive content provider in China, can also be attributed to internet technology.

Advertising, search engines, e-commerce and online gaming are the four principal internet revenue streams. The launch of 3G in early 2009 significantly increased the popularity of mobile devices and has shaped new trends in mobile internet. The huge growth of mobile phone users has precipitated a new round of internet use. According to statistics from the Ministry of Industry and Information Technology, China had 384 million net users at the end of 2009. However, despite the fact that Chinese net users account for almost a third its total population, internet access in China is still low compared with the United States and Japan where net use accounts for 77.3 and 78.2 per cent of the total population respectively.[1] Statistics from the Ministry of Industry and Information Technology of P.R. China also show that by end of Sept 2010, telephone users in

---

[1] See http://www.internetworldstats.com/stats.htm [accessed 21 March 2011].

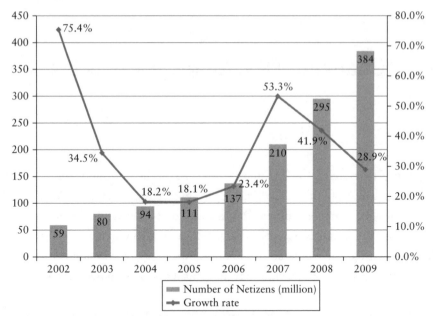

Figure 3.1 The Scale and Growth Rate of Chinese Netizens
Source: Chinese Ministry of Industry and Information Technology, Statistical data 2010

China reached 1.13 billion including 300 million landline users and 830 million mobile phone users. Broadband users increased to 110 million in 2010.[2]

Integrated development

In a 2002 research paper I identified three development trends of modern industries: industrial clusters, industrial convergence and industrial ecology.[3] I called for the elimination of institutional fragmentation to allow the growth of new forms of industry.

As a new industrial development model creative industries challenge conventional economic development models. The significance of this extends far beyond being a new industrial form. It lies in the innovation of the economic system, optimization of industrial structures, an increase in the competitiveness of regions and the construction of a creative society.

[2] Statistics from the Ministry of Industry and Information Technology of P.R.China. *China Daily*, 29 June 2010. http://www.chinadaily.com.cn/hqgj/jryw/2010-06-29/content_512367.html [accessed 8 March 2011].
[3] Wuwei Li and Huimin Wang (2002), 'Rational Thinking and Prediction on Industrial Development Trends,' *China Industrial Economics*, 2, 27–30.

Creative industries are a combination of science and technology, culture, industry and the market. This crossover is a basic characteristic of many new types of industries. The concept of cross-boundary convergence requires us to challenge tradition by overcoming fragmentation of industries, and by achieving integration of resources.

Integration is a challenge for government coordination and management. Overcoming boundaries between sectors and achieving coordinated, cross-sector development are key practical issues. I believe that once the approach is changed, government and companies will discover new growth opportunities in modern service industries. Likewise, manufacturing industries will undergo transformation. Highly personalized new products, new services, new technologies, and new business models will be generated.

The establishment of a high-level cross-sector coordinating system is an approach taken in China and elsewhere. For instance, when Britain proposed the creative industries strategy in 1998, the then Prime Minister Tony Blair was the chairman of the Creative Industries Task Force. In Hong Kong, the former Chief Executive Tung Chee-hwa was the one in charge of Hong Kong's creative industries program. In Beijing coordination and management operates through the Beijing Cultural and Creative Industries Leadership Group and its permanent establishment, the Beijing Cultural and Creative Industries Promotion Centre. The Party Secretary of Beijing Liu Qi is the leader of the Group and Mayor Wang Qishan is the deputy leader. Since its establishment in 2006, the Promotion Centre has played an effective cross-sector management role and carried out a series of initiatives to promote cultural and creative industries. These initiatives include formulating development plans, implementation of policies, the designation of cultural and creative industries clusters and training bases, research on policy implementation, coordination and organization of key research projects, establishment of public service platforms, and international exchange and cooperation.

Beyond Cultural Industries

Cultural industries, content industries, copyright industries, and creative industries are often regarded as being similar. Creative industries however were born out of cultural industries and yet they extend beyond cultural industries; they are shaped by innovative industrial practices with a direct relationship to individual creativity and intellectual property. In comparison with cultural industries more emphasis is placed on integration with primary, secondary and tertiary industries.

The emergence of creative industries policy reveals top-down development strategies closely connected to cultural fields; in addition, government policies have aimed to promote local economic, cultural and social progress and make local industries nationally competitive. Sectors related to culture formed the main content of creative industries policy at an earlier stage; the UK definition of creative industries subsequently became the benchmark for many countries and regions in developing their strategies. From the various definitions and categories of creative industries across the world, we can now identify three common aspirations:

- to utilize creativity in products;

- to generate product value through the use of symbolic meanings;

- to make intellectual property a key asset protected by law.

From the existing categorizations we can see that the scope of activities is both broad and complex. Apart from sectors that have come about as a result of new technology, most creative activities have existed for a long time. Therefore, creative industries are not one specific industry but are a group of industrial categories that share similar characteristics in their contribution to social and cultural development, which have similar potential for economic development and employment, and enjoy special attention from government. They not only include industries whose operational mechanism is based on economic and material capital, but also emerging industries that operate on intellectual capital, cultural capital and social capital.

Creative Industries vs. Traditional Industries

Our understanding of creative industries is not confined by the logic of 'traditional' industries. We should examine the meaning and essential nature of creative industries against a background of technological progress, industry convergence and transformation in consumption. There are significant differences between creative industries and traditional industries (see Table 3.1). Creative

Table 3.1 Comparison of Development Logic in Traditional Industries and Creative Industries

	Traditional Industries	Creative Industries
Driver	Hard capital (land, financial capital etc)	Soft capital (knowledge, culture, human resource etc)
Resource	Single use	Repeatable use
Chain	Linear production chain	Circle value chain
Organization	Vertical structure	Flat structure
Orientation	Product value	Consumer value
Revenue	Increasing marginal cost, diminishing marginal revenue	Diminishing marginal cost, increasing marginal revenue
Goal	Economic development	Economic, social and human development

industries highlight the role of soft factors such as culture and human resources; they emphasize repeated and intensive use of resources, have a consumer-centred focus, organizational flexibility and a diversity of industry targets.

This mode of innovative thinking manifests as creative agriculture when applied to traditional agricultural activities; architectural design when applied to construction and environmental planning (architecture, landscape, interior decoration, community planning, exhibition, industrial parks, urban environment, modern business districts, commercial centres, land and sea transportation, bridge engineering and municipal engineering design); and creative tourism when applied to tourism. In this the tourism industrial chain is extended into a cross-sector, multi-level industrial chain to stimulate the transformation of regions through integration with primary and secondary industries. The convergence of creative industries makes it possible to integrate technology and culture with the market so as to extend and expand the development of industries.

Concept of Value Innovation

In an article I wrote in 2007, I pointed out that creative industries are an important means to achieve the Blue Ocean Strategy.[4] As mentioned in chapter one, the cornerstone of the Blue Ocean is value innovation. Likewise, the core development concept of creative industries is value innovation through the application of new ways of thinking to existing industries. In some senses value innovation represents a fundamental change in the concept of wealth creation. This change is reflected in the new logic of value creation: from product innovation to value innovation, from function value to concept value, and from the Red Ocean to the Blue Ocean.

From product innovation to value innovation

To surf in the Blue Ocean does not necessarily imply that we must look for business opportunities in completely unknown industries. On the contrary, we can also discover a 'blue area' in the Red Ocean. The key is to change the way of thinking by turning from product innovation to value innovation which enables exploration of both the known and the unknown market space. An INSEAD study of more than 100 new business projects finds that 86 per cent of these projects are in the Red Ocean industries and only 14 per cent are Blue Ocean projects. But these Blue Ocean projects eventually contribute 61 per cent of the business profits.[5] This shows us that the Blue Ocean Strategy is the starting point and practice for innovation of business models with a core strategy of value innovation. The key to success is to provide products and services that can provide unprecedented value for consumers.

Then how to provide new value elements for consumers? The answer is for creative industries to penetrate into and integrate with various industries. We can say that creative industries are a means of achieving the Blue Ocean Strategy.

From use value to symbolic value

Demand is the driving force behind the formation of value. From a consumer perspective the value of a product consists of both its use value and its symbolic

---

[4] Wuwei Li (2007). 'Creative Industries: The Key to Enter into Blue Ocean', *Wenhui Bao*, 7 Sep 2007.

[5] Kim, W. Chan and Mauborgne, R. *Blue Ocean Strategy: How to Creative Uncontested Market Space and Make the Competition Irrelevant*. (Cambridge: Harvard Business School Press, 2005).

value. Use value is the price a consumer is willing to pay for the physical properties of goods so as to satisfy their own basic needs. Symbolic value refers to the price a consumer is willing to pay for the feelings and experiences brought about by the cultural elements and the symbolic meaning embedded in the goods, on top of the price paid for the functional value.[6] For instance, if an enterprise makes two leather bags of the same design using the same leather material and sews the Louis Vuitton brand to one bag and a general brand to the other, the market price of the 'LV' bag will be more than ten times that of the other. There is a legendary story behind the Louis Vuitton brand. An ordinary cobbler was selected by the French king Louis XIII for his craftsmanship to serve the royal family. The cobbler used the best material and made the best products. Because of this royal association, the symbolic meaning of owning a Louis Vuitton bag relates to concepts of privilege and wealth. By satisfying certain psychological needs of consumers, the Louis Vuitton brand has comparatively high symbolic value.[7]

With economic development and increased income, the shift of focus from use value to symbolic value increases product value and consumer awareness. Manufacturers apply storytelling, symbols and other elements (the brand for instance) to the production and consumption of products. When products become carriers of cultural meaning, their symbolic value is significantly increased.

As shown in Figure 3.2, the increase of concept value can expand demand and create a new market in the Blue Ocean.

From the Red Ocean to the Blue Ocean

For a long time competition and competitive advantage have been major concerns in the strategic management of companies. Guided by Michael Porter's competitive strategic thinking, companies often choose either a strategy of

---

[6] These intangible elements are subjective.

[7] From a consumer perspective, creative industries create concept value to occupy the market and to make profits by way of using new creative ideas to improve the concept value of products. In contrast to traditional industries characterized by the product-oriented value creation mechanism, creative industries are demand-oriented and customers are both the starting point and the end point of value creation. The value innovation is achieved by means of satisfying customers' cultural demand.

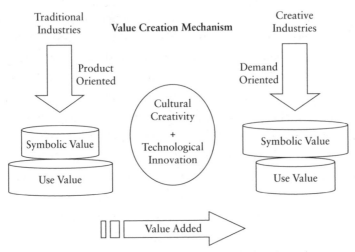

Figure 3.2 The Value Creation Mechanism of Creative Industries

'differentiation' or one of 'lower cost.' They aim to beat their rivals and grab a greater market share. But stimulated by globalization and information technology, the rate of technological diffusion has increased. A large number of homogeneous products have flooded the market and competition has become more intense. The market occupied by companies, the known market space, is the result of intense competition leading to reduced profits and shrinking markets. When many companies carve up market share in competition with each other, this results in a Red Ocean. This metaphor describes the nature of much global competition.

Creative industries are the key to entering into the Blue Ocean not only because they can provide symbolic value for consumers but also because they are capable of penetrating into and integrating with a variety of other industries. This integration of technology, culture, manufacturing, and services helps the growth of industries and the expansion of development space for urban industries. Industries brought about by technology, especially information technology, are showing great vitality which is manifested in their penetration into and integration with traditional cultural industries as well as in high growth. At the same time, the broad application of information technology and the change in the mode of production have led to the breaking down of boundaries between various traditional cultural sectors. This in turn has led to more penetration and integration between various sectors and has turned the concept of market regions into the concept of market place.

The creative industries are a broad industrial group; their output can be transformed into inputs for other industries. Mickey Mouse, Barbie, Harry Potter, Mashimaro, and Hello Kitty are all outputs of this kind. Since the brands were established, they have penetrated extensively into other industries, such as toys, stationery, clothes and accessories, baggage, and food, and have significantly increased the value added of these industries. In addition, music can be recorded to chips that can be integrated into other products to increase their value. Creative marketing can help almost all traditional industries to enter into Blue Ocean and promote the development of a number of related industries.

Concept of People-oriented Development

Diversification is one of the prominent features of creative industries, and stands in contrast to the single economic objective of many traditional industries. Creative industries shift the focus of the development of resources from the object to the subject or more specifically, towards individual creativity. The significance of this shift lies not only in a view of creativity as a precious top-end resource or the ability to turn new ideas into saleable products and services but also in the overall concept of creative industries. Creative industries advocate the release of human potential and the realization of self worth to make people feel happy about their efforts and bring about a return to 'people-oriented' values. In this context, what creative industries advocate is a concept of people-oriented development. This development concept has not only changed the value orientation of economic development but also created a new lifestyle combining work with entertainment.

From economic growth to economic development

Growth and development are two different concepts. The transformation from economic growth to economic development is a conceptual change. The objective of development is of benefit to the general population. Economic growth and material wealth can have real social value and human significance only when they are achieved under an economic and social development strategy that aims at promoting the development of everyone in society. As Richard Florida points out 'our society continues to encourage the creative talents of a minority, while neglecting the creative capacities of many more. Addressing these issues goes beyond an intellectual or social agenda; it is required work if we wish to generate long-term prosperity by aligning economic growth with the fuller development of human potential.'

Economic growth focuses on quantity. It relates to the increased output caused by variations in input. The connotation of economic development, however, is broader and deeper than simple economic growth. It relates to systemic changes: from small to big, from simple to complex, and from lower to higher. It represents a combination of quantitative and qualitative changes that include not only transformations in production inputs but also elements which are the driving forces of development: structure, quality, efficiency, employment, distribution, consumption, ecology, and environment. Economic development encompasses economic growth whereas economic growth does not necessarily encompass economic development. Economic development not only pays attention to economic scale and improvements in efficiency but to coordination of economic systems, sustainability of development and the sharing of development results. Economic growth is more output-oriented and is focused on the pursuit of quantity and the expansion of scale. It is unsustainable if it is in blind pursuit of high growth at the cost of ecological damage. When economic growth lacks a humanistic approach, it will fall into the trap of pure growth and lose sight of its original objectives.

Creative industries promote human development while promoting economic growth. As defined by DCMS: 'The creative industries are those industries that are based on individual creativity, skill and talent. They are also those that have the potential to create wealth and jobs through developing intellectual property'.[8] The core capital of creative industries is individual creativity. Individual talent and skills can become new highlights of economic growth in modern economic development by generating wealth. It is very important that everyone should have the opportunity to realize their talents. Individual creativity should be inspired. It is going to be a powerful force in promoting social and economic progress as well as representing a huge potential for change in China's economic development model. In the near future, creative industries will become strategic industries that will give free rein to the creative talent of the Chinese people and improve their quality of life.

[8] http://www.culture.gov.uk/what_we_do/creative_industries/default.aspx [accessed 8 March 2011].

I once wrote an article on this topic entitled 'Creativity is not the Sole Ownership of a Master.'[9] I argued that 'the wisdom of three cobblers is worth that of a master'. Today, the internet provides a convenient communication channel and enables creative output to be rapidly transformed into productivity, wealth and even employment. In the course of this process, the social value of the individual, whether he is a celebrity or an ordinary person, can be realized and individual self development furthered.

Economic growth is only a means, not an end in itself. The promotion of human progress is the fundamental purpose of economic development. In a society relatively rich in material resources, cultural demand is on the rise. Creative industries can provide products the cultural entertainment function of which provide a model of development for humankind featuring the double 'dividends' of cultural and material benefit.

From object resources to subject resources

Resource is a broad concept which includes the material and the intangible. Intangible resources consist of the accumulated wealth of human knowledge, including cultural heritage, human thoughts and scientific achievement. Material resources are tangible resources provided by nature, such as minerals, land and resources in the form of factory buildings, farmland and energy. Generally speaking, resources developed and utilized by conventional traditional industries are largely material. Creative industries, on the other hand, focus on the development of intangible assets: they convert intangible resources into capital, thereby promoting economic development. This kind of regenerated capital is characterized by low consumption and high value added.

Intangible resources are capable of being transformed into development capital in order to bring about economic benefits. Folk legends and elements of social life, for instance, are resources which can be developed and used for economic growth. The *Harry Potter* series is a classic example. Statistics show that the economic turnover of industries related to *Harry Potter* is over US$200 billion.

---

[9] Wuwei Li, 'Creativity is not the Sole Ownership of a Master,' *Wenhui Bao*, 22 Mar 2006.

In the age of the material economy, hard capital occupied the dominant position. If you had land, factory buildings and money, you held competitive advantage. In the age of the creative economy, soft capital becomes the key factor in obtaining competitive advantage. For instance, a brand is soft capital with high value added. Owning a brand can occupy more market share and bring profits that exceed those of land, factory buildings and labour. In the knowledge economy, social capital, information capital, cultural capital and intellectual capital are the important factors in production. There are structural changes in the core drivers of some new industries. Intangible capital has become the main capital form of the new industries. The core capital of creative industries consists of knowledge and wisdom rather than labour and raw materials in the traditional sense.

With economic and social development, the form of capital is also evolving. The shift in human development from material to intangible resources is inevitable. Material resources are limited whereas intangibles are infinite. South Korea promoted the idea of 'limited resources, unlimited creativity.' From the perspective of development, the development and application of intangibles is in accordance with the scientific concept of low pollution and high output.

Creative capital can be used repeatedly and infinitely. In other words, creative capital can represent one input and multiple outputs. The content value of creative products can be repeatedly consumed and used. Examples include Shakespeare's classic *Hamlet*, Hugo's *Les Miserables*, China's *Dream of Red Mansions* and *Butterfly Lovers*. The passage of time has not affected the content. By means of modern technology, these beautiful stories can be made into opera, ballet, comics and local dramas. They can also be made into films, recorded on CDs, and even adapted into animations to expand their economic value. The ancient Chinese story of *Hua Mulan* was used by Disney to make a bestselling animated movie.

Once a movie is successful it can reap profit in sales of DVDs, videos, TV rights, souvenirs, and clothes and accessories. In the animation industry, the ratio of the original product and its merchandising can reach 1:3 or even 1:5. Disney's animation productions have theme parks, consumer goods and media products attached to them. The Disney characters appear on books, stationery, food, clothes, and toys. The price of a consumer good with the logo of a cute Mickey Mouse is much higher than that of a similar consumer good without that logo. Statistics show that audio-visual products may generate income from merchandising four times that of the original products. This means that the product value of US$500,000–600,000 can generate US$2 million in merchandising.[10]

Creative capital can quickly generate large-scale profits. Advertising, architecture, arts and antiques, crafts, design, film, interactive leisure software, music, performing arts, publishing, software, broadcasting, games and online games, animation, DV, Flash, SMS, and mobile video, rely on creative ideas. Dissemination and marketing rely even more on technology which can rapidly distribute products and stimulate new waves of consumption. High returns on investment can be accumulated in a short period of time.

From working hard to working happily

In *The Rise of the Creative Class*, Richard Florida coined the 3T concept (Technology, Talent and Tolerance). The 'creative class' is the generic term for people working in occupations that utilize creativity. It includes scientists and engineers, poets, artists, designers, health and law practitioners, and people working in hi-tech and knowledge-intensive industries. In China these people are called '*xinxin renlei*' or 'new human beings' who have new ideas and different attitudes towards life. Their creative spirit and risk-taking are having a positive influence on the younger generation; their work and activities constitute the most dynamic elements of urban landscapes; their lifestyles and values are impacting on the development of cities and communities. With numbers on the rise, more changes are expected to future lifestyles and working cultures.

Creative talents

The development of creative industries relies on creative abilities. Ability and intellectual property are the source and core of the creative industries value chain. Lack of innovative ability has become one of the bottlenecks in the development of creative industries. At present, China's cultural and creative

---

[10] Xavier Greffe, X. (2008), '*New Business Models for Culture*,' Conference paper at Griffith University, Australia. Oct. 2008. http://www.griffith.edu.au/__data/assets/pdf_file/0016/100645/Greffe-Seminar2-Text.pdf

industries are lacking in people who are not only familiar with the content of cultural and creative industries but who are also good at management and operations. In other words, people with skills in commercialization and marketing are in high demand. But what kind of skill sets do creative industries need? How are they to be cultivated? The solution is education, innovative education.

John Howkins says, 'The most important factor in a creative economy is education. There is a high correlation between a country's education level and the size and strength of its creative economy.'[11] Establishing an innovative education system should be addressed as a national strategy with a view to revitalizing national cultural industries.

Creative ideas can be copied and money can be returned on bank loans. But creative skills are hard to find. Creative industries are an industrialized business operation system covering the process of creative planning, production, marketing and consumption. Designers, production crews, agents, marketing professionals and managers are all professionally trained.

What society really needs is a combination of creative skills and practical capabilities. Richard Florida points out that every creative person in today's society should have three educational qualifications or receive three levels of education. The three-level education refers to art education, technology education and business-related training. People with this educational background will form the competitive and innovative skill base needed in today's environment.

The success of creative industries over the past decade in developed countries such as Britain and Australia can be attributed to an emphasis on the cultivation of creative skills. The London Business School and The University of the Arts London have been collaborating to train people in arts and management. The Greater London Authority has invested 50 million pounds in this program in which students of the two educational institutions are trained together. The cultural and creative industries in the United States are global leaders. More than thirty universities offer arts management courses and produce a large number of graduates with degrees in planning, marketing and management.

---

[11] John Howkins' Introduction to Li Wuwei's book *Creative Industries are Changing China*, China: Xinhua Press 2009, p. 6.

In Australia, the Queensland University of Technology (QUT) established the world's first Faculty of Creative Industries in 2001. The faculty offers interdisciplinary courses that cover more than a dozen disciplines and combine creative arts (e.g. performing arts, media and journalism) with IT-based design (e.g. fashion, games and media design). These courses are also combined respectively with education, law, business and IT to provide joint-degree education. In addition, the faculty offers various short-term training courses and summer school programs related to the creative industries. The teaching curriculum focuses on applied courses and aims at meeting the employment market demand. It provides a balanced education and training in both theory and practice. Because of this, QUT is known as 'a university for the real world.' The university has the largest number of graduates each year and its graduate employment rate is well above the national average for Australian universities.

China's tertiary education is not far behind. In recent years, around sixty universities nationwide have provided courses related to cultural and creative industries. Animation and games are the fastest growing sectors of these courses. All this has effectively alleviated the talent shortage in terms of quantity. However, there is an imbalance with a scarcity of high-end creative skills. As we know, cultural and creative industries are inter-disciplinary, combining elements of culture, arts, economics, management, and science and technology. They are both broad-based and highly specialized. Universities and research institutions should provide targeted education for different levels of talent in design, production, management, marketing, and research by taking advantage of the rich resources of creative disciplines and exploring the potential of interdisciplinary education.

The Communication University of China (CUC), a top university of media and communication in China, is an important training ground for creative industries. Its curriculum, approach and educational philosophy provide a teaching model for other Chinese universities. CUC makes sure that its courses are at the forefront of the industry and can cater to industry specifications and market demand. Its courses in creative media, international cultural trade and cultural industry management reflect industry sectors in urgent need of new skills. CUC's three-level bachelor, masters and PhD degrees coupled with the effort to open the university to creative practitioners and business leaders to expand networking and to share ideas and experiences is catering to the demand for innovative and capable marketing and management skills which have risen in demand as a result of the emergence of creative industries.

Peking University has had success in nurturing practical skills. It has a collaborative training program with Time-Warner to produce marketing and management personnel for the cultural industries. This project adopts a 'full-interaction' teaching and practice mode which includes case studies, market surveys, research reports, simulation exercises and experiments. In both simulated and real situations, students put into practice their knowledge and skills under the guidance of successful industry professionals. This kind of training highlights the importance of practical skills.

In 2005, the Shanghai Theatre Academy (STA) established the School of Creative Studies, the first of its kind in China. The school offers specialized courses in creative skills which include management, gaming and animation, creative media, and visual communication. The School of Creative Studies has been actively engaged in the construction of a discipline system and has broken out of the traditional teaching model and established a base of teaching, research, and production for creative education. It provides various kinds of practice bases and platforms for students to consolidate and deepen their classroom knowledge, develop their personality, improve their practical skills and potential for innovation.

The formation of the creative class relies on a tolerant diversified culture and an enabling social environment. The development of creative education needs a collaborative approach: government support, corporate coaching, tertiary education, and private education. We need to further expand social tolerance and create a more relaxed cultural environment if we are to encourage bold and controversial creative ideas. This will help liberate the workers in the creative industries from ideological restraints and activate their creativity.

Creative education is a systematic project. It needs the collaborated effort of educational institutions, business and the community for its coordinated development. Innovative education will pave the way for China's march towards the creative economy.

4

Changing the Approach to Value Creation

Xintiandi is a popular attraction in Shanghai, blending history and culture. The renovated street area in the downtown French Concession district draws together tourism, restaurant dining, business, entertainment and lifestyle. By integrating the design of traditional stone-gated tenement buildings (*shikumen*) with modern architecture, the old alleys have been transformed into recreational and entertainment venues. The renovation has injected new life into the historical tenement buildings. While Xintiandi gives the appearance of a cluster of old buildings its functionality is modern; a strong feeling of modernity exudes the richness of Shanghai culture, the integration of Eastern and Western cultures and a combination of traditional and modern cultures. It is a place of nostalgia for the elderly, fashion for the young, Western lifestyle for the Chinese and Chinese culture for foreigners.

Shikumen and Shanghai Rice Wine form an ideal complement. A product of the Shanghai Jinfeng Wine Company Limited which has a history dating back to 1939, Shanghai Rice Wine was sold at three yuan a bottle. Later, the company generated a new wine product and adopted a creative, modern approach to brand building. It built up an association with nostalgia, using the symbolism of Shikumen while utilizing modern concepts to redesign the packaging. When Shanghai Shikumen Rice Wine was launched it was a market success; a large part of the success was because the brand strategy is not simply rice wine, but wine culture, namely the nostalgic feelings associated with living in Shikumen buildings and the tastes of a younger generation for both Chinese and Western cultural elements.

The Shikumen alleys in Shanghai are lined with traditional stone-gated buildings, a combination of Eastern and Western cultures. But more importantly these are a symbol of Shanghai culture. They provide historical witness to the customs, habits and stories of various historical periods. Taking advantage of these legacies, the Shanghai Shikumen Holiday Hotel opened in May 2005 as a hotel chain. Its aim was to extend the cultural environment associated with the Shikumen buildings and to provide a unique experience of Shanghai culture.

Likewise, Shanghai Shikumen Restaurant is a franchise specializing in Shanghai cuisine. It provides a modern environment blended with traditional local cultural elements as well as generating innovations in traditional Shanghai cuisine.

The Shikumen symbolism demonstrates how successful creative brands can utilize rich cultural resources. Creative brands value personality and individuality and utilize emotional associations; they can inspire imagination and association in consumers. The transformation of historical and cultural resources into business resources requires creativity. This can be achieved in a number of ways.

First, consumers are more likely to accept cultural elements contained in historical resources if the original forms are developed in accordance with the times. This is achieved by integrating modern elements and historical resources, by replacing old with new. If Xintiandi had no modern elements, it would not have attracted so many visitors. Modern technology assists in the process of replacing the old with the new.

Second, many stories are contained within historical and cultural resources and these can be activated through the power of storytelling. The interpretation of stories in various forms and formats disseminates the cultural meanings of historical resources. Telling stories in a creative way integrates original resources, which are waiting to be developed, activating and adding value to these resources. The Shanghai Shikumen Rice Wine is an example of using creativity in brand building through a combination of history, wine culture and music.

A third way is to create emotional responses. Consumer brand recognition and the eventual purchase of a product is a process of changing emotions. To influence consumers and to make them purchase a product is 'the most thrilling leap' for a business. Creativity comes from life, so the generation of good creative ideas must start with an understanding of the psychology of target consumers, especially their emotional needs. The connection point between the product and the consumer's emotions and feelings can then be located and eventually an association can be established between the product or brand and those emotions and feelings. The success of the Shikumen series can be attributed to the exploitation of consumer nostalgia and identification with and attachment to Shanghai culture.

Finally, intellectual property recognition is important for the protection of rights and interests. Creative industries demonstrate that wealth and employment are generated through intellectual property. Many creative and cultural outputs are easy to copy because of the nature of their material manifestations. They, therefore, need intellectual property protection. In addition, intellectual property is a business tool; it is very important to establish and manage intellectual property when developing historical and cultural resources. Doing so not only protects entitlements but also allows the development of various business activities such as franchises, affiliated shops, OEM production, and transfer transactions.

The Value System of Creative Industries

The value system of creative industries is expressed through two channels. One benefits from the interpenetration and integration of various industries and industry sectors. The other is the benefit of scale brought about by global, creative value-focused restructuring or integration of value modules. Both models require the combination of creativity, technology, products and markets; they also require the establishment of core industries, supporting industries, related industries, and merchandising industries.

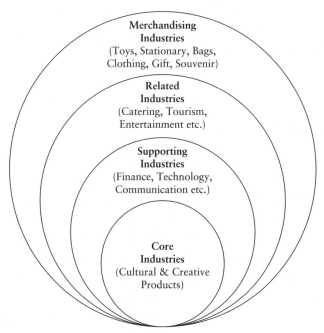

Merchandising Industries
(Toys, Stationary, Bags, Clothing, Gift, Souvenir)

Related Industries
(Catering, Tourism, Entertainment etc.)

Supporting Industries
(Finance, Technology, Communication etc.)

Core Industries
(Cultural & Creative Products)

Figure 4.1 Value System of Creative Industries

This four-level value system is the ideal model for industrializing cultural creativity and maximizing value.

Core industries

The core industries are those enterprises that continue to generate creative products. They aspire to value innovation; they lead in the distribution and extension of the value chain. The core industries are also the brand or the main products of an enterprise. Creative industries could not develop without core industries.

Supporting industries

Supporting industries are those enterprise groups that directly support production, development and dissemination of creative products. They provide elements and services for the core industries. They include enterprises in the fields of science and technology, finance, media and advertising.

Related industries

Though not directly supporting the production of creative products, related industries provide an enabling environment for the development of the creative industries, particularly in fostering a creative workforce and in promoting and marketing products. Related industry sectors engage in tourism, catering, bar and night clubs, entertainment and training as well as logistics, marketing, design, processing and production of industrial R&D.

Merchandising industries

Merchandising industries provide value-added services and products, such as toys, stationery, clothes and accessories, luggage, food and souvenirs. The more developed merchandising industries are, the further the industrial chain will extend. The wealth created by merchandising industries can exceed that of the core industries, the supporting industries and the related industries.

The clustering of core industries produces a stronger demand for both upstream and downstream related industries in the industrial chain. This demand boosts the development of these industries and then, at some point, helps to establish a new, complete industrial chain. This effect functions like roots crops: it generates multiplier benefits through a process of division, expansion and growth.

The Value Adding of Creativity

The multiplier benefits of creative industries come from a comprehensive industrial value system. A good example is the acrobatic extravaganza 'Era'. This multimedia spectacular, which was produced and performed by the Shanghai Acrobatic Troupe, broke market boundaries. Not only was the audience amazed by the acrobats' control and precision, they were enchanted by a world created by multimedia, technology, lighting and sound effects, elaborate costumes, and original live music. The combination of acrobatics and creativity made the show a real hit. Era illustrated the value-adding model of integrating creativity and technology with tourism products. Here, the core industries are the evolving creative tourism project companies jointly launched by Shanghai Media Group, China Arts Corporation, Shanghai Acrobatic Troupe and Shanghai Circus. The result is a creative product that has dominated the value chain. The supporting industries are the enterprise groups that have directly supported the production, development and dissemination of the creative tourism product. They are engaged in technology, finance, media and advertising. The related industries and the merchandising industries have all played a role in the commercial success of Era. Apart from box office income of 100 million yuan, Era has also reaped more than two million yuan from merchandising.

From Cultural Resources to Business Resources

The most prominent characteristic of creative industries is the encouragement of the infinite release of individual creativity. This creates new products and new market demand by breaking through the hard constraints of material resources. Individual creativity can turn cultural resources into business resources by transforming cultural resources into capital and market. In doing so new channels and new market places will be opened for economic development. It is in these transformations that creative industries are able to rise and develop and to help transform the mode of economic development.

From the perspective of economics, the concept of 'resources' contains the following elements:

First, resources are the combination of various factors that can create wealth or assets. This means that all material, cultural and institutional factors, including human knowledge and talent, social capital, science and technology, and culture are resources. Second, the transformation of resources into wealth is achieved by human labour. Third, resources are the sum of various factors that already exist which can be developed and used. Resources exist in three forms: abandoned resources, available resources and potential resources. Resources not only exist in different material forms but include intangible information resources such as knowledge, experience and technology.

In the traditional economy, labour, natural resources and capital are the main contributors to economic growth; the role played by human capital depends on the existence and utilization of resources. In the age of the knowledge economy, the leading resources will experience epoch-making changes in economic development, that is human resources and knowledge will become the leading resources and drivers of economic development. When human creativity becomes the leading resource, the definition of what constitutes a resource is broadened and extended to include repositories of historical material, folk legends, customs and traditions, stories and tales which can be developed into useful resources for economic growth. The transformation from cultural to business resources not only promotes coordinated, sustainable economic development but also creates cultural brands and promotes national culture.

The old tenement buildings in Shanghai are structures of historical significance. They are not simply 'architectural artworks' and a kind of architectural heritage unique to Shanghai. They are also bearers of history and culture. As residential buildings representing a certain historical period, the tenement buildings are a microcosm of the social life of Shanghai. Now a symbol of Shanghai culture, the tenement buildings are used by other industries to add cultural value to products so as to associate products with particular feelings. This has helped product promotion and helped the successful transformation from cultural resource to business resource. The symbolic value of tenement buildings in Shanghai is a showcase of 'one source, multi-uses', the multiplied-benefits business model of creative industries.

Creative Tourism

Creative tourism is a recent development model for tourism industries globally. Its emergence is the inevitable effect of a market shift from the 'era of mass tourism' to the 'era of mass leisure' and now to the 'era of personal experience.'

It is also a sign of the desire of tourism to position itself within the knowledge economy. Creative tourism establishes a cross-sector, multi-level industrial chain of tourism by integrating primary and secondary industries as well as expanding the range of activities and attractions. Such expansion stimulates the transformation of regions. Compared with the established development model of tourism, creative tourism has the following characteristics:

The multi-dimensional integration of resources

Creative tourism accords special attention to the integration and transformation of social resources in addition to resources such as natural landscapes and cultural heritage. It seeks to apply creative strategies to transform tangible and intangible resources into marketable products. Creativity is a means of transforming resources into capital and it is also a way for the tourism industries to develop, exploit and integrate resources more deeply and more extensively.

The creation of future cultural heritage

Generally speaking tourism industries develop, utilize and protect historical, as well as existing tourism resources. While China has expended large amounts of financial and material resources on repairing and developing historical sites there is often little attention paid to creativity. As a result, there are few world-class innovative products. From the perspective of creative industries, tourism products are attractions that showcase creative human activities. Areas which lack natural tourism resources need to focus on the production of future cultural heritage. Accordingly, creating tourist attractions for the future is a basic starting point for creative tourism.

Guiding and creating consumer trends in tourism

China's tourism industries tend to have two points of focus: resources and market. The first is the practice of developing products based on natural resources. Scenic spots are the core attraction as well as the industry focus. This kind of tourism operates from the logic of resources. The market-oriented approach arises from the tendency to 'follow the market.' When 'planning cannot catch up with 'changes' in the market, which is often the case, there

Table 4.1 Model Comparison: Traditional Tourism vs. Creative Tourism

	Traditional Tourism	Creative Tourism
Tourist	• Inexperienced • Unsophisticated • In group	• Sophisticated • Experienced • Differentiated
Orientation	Resource-oriented and market-oriented	Leading market and consumer-oriented
Resource	Natural scenery, landscape, historical and cultural heritage	Tangible and intangible social resources
Driver	Hard-factor	Soft-factor
Competition	Price competition	Innovation competition
Product Feature	• Popular for mass market • Separated activities • Single activity • Seasonal tourism	• Personalized for niche market • Integrated activities • Comprehensive tourism activities • All-season tourism
Industry Boundary	With boundary	Without boundary
Management	Separated	Modularly integrated
Value	Value added for related products	Value added for the entire value system
Goal	Single goal (economic development)	Multiple goals (environmental, economic and social development)

is often loss of investment and waste of resources. It is natural, therefore, for creative tourism to become the new development; creative tourism focuses on the stimulation of potential demand and on consumer trends. Creative tourism strives to integrate 'markets and creativity', producing high value added, a 'cool' industrial model.

The expansion and extension of the industrial chain to improve the overall value of a region

Traditionally tourism industries are categorized as service industries. Six elements – travel, shopping, transportation, catering, entertainment and accommodation – are seen as constituting the core tourism activities. The industrial chain includes information and financial services; the value realization of tourism products is, however, the focus. Creative tourism establishes a cross-sector, multi-level industrial chain by expanding the range of activities and attractions and by taking the initiative to integrate with primary and secondary industries. The aim is to stimulate, improve and transform the functionality of a region.

New Values of Creative Tourism

Tourism in the age of personalized experience needs to create experiential tourism products. What people really look for is not simply a leisure and holiday package to please the body and the soul; they look for personalized tourism products with distinctive features to enrich their journey and experiences.

'Play' has become an economic resources for an individual, an industry and even a nation. Driven by this trend of 'pleasure-oriented consumption,' an increasing number of products and services have begun to provide entertainment functions or to combine with entertainment activities: the 'play economy' is no longer limited to certain specific and bounded industries. Everything is done in 'another way' to make it 'more fun.' 'Another way' represents a new way of thinking and a new perspective. Here, creativity plays a key role in creating 'another way.' In the 'play economy,' there are no trend followers: it depends on what new tricks you can come up with; continuous innovation and pre-empting trends are very important.

Creative tourism aims to bring about smart growth. In order to do this in China it needs to promote cross-boundary development and achieve seamless linkages and healthy interactions between industries. The expansion of the tourism industrial chain needs to focus on breaking through the limited cycle of the 'six elements of tourism'. To achieve this, tourism industries need to take advantage of the experiential demand of the entertainment age and make creative tourism an 'input factor' and 'value-added capital' for business growth. In this way, creative tourism becomes a key link in various industries' effort to increase the value added (to realize the experiential value). This also enables interaction and integration between tourism and related industries.

Second, consumption stimulates feedback mechanisms that improve performance. The idea of creative tourism provides a broad market base and a leading role in the transformation from 'Made in China' to 'Created in China.' It enables the upgrading of manufacturing industries into a virtuous circle of consumption – production – consumption. To be specific, tourism functions are extended into the various links throughout the industrial chain, especially into upstream R&D and the downstream sales channels of brands. Consumer demand can be used to guide product design and functional optimization. Consumer preference can be taken into account in brand positioning. Loyal consumer groups can be cultivated and effective sales networks established. Meanwhile, potential consumer demand should be the focus of new industrial spaces. For instance, the development of water tourism activities such as yachting, cruise ships and pleasure boats enables new industries including the manufacturing and design industries of special equipments for yachts and cruise ships and the manufacturing, decoration and repair industries for water sports equipment.

Expanding the 'spatial chain': cross-regional joint development

Creative tourism pays attention to the improvement in the overall value of a region. This is typical of what we call the 'new wooden barrel' thinking. The old wooden barrel theory states that the capacity of a wooden barrel is determined not by the longest wooden board but the shortest. It illustrates the need for special attention to the strengthening of the shortest board. In contrast, the new wooden barrel theory concentrates on the creation of a bigger barrel space by combining the longest board of the wooden barrel with the longest wooden board of other barrels (or other regions). Likewise, by expanding into other regions the tourism industry chain can expect to achieve joint development across administrative regions and to optimize the distribution of tourism industrial resources in a larger geographical area.

The Yangzi River Delta region is a good example of a 'spatial chain'. Unbalanced development and non-homogeneous features exist in the region.

A solution is to position the functions of the different cities in this region and establish a tourist destination system with differential strategies. For instance, taking advantage of the natural spaces in the region, a number of competitive, cross-regional tourism clusters would achieve a rational spatial layout, such as a Yangzi River tourism zone, a Taihu Lake tourism zone, a Grand Canal tourism zone, and an East China Sea coastal tourism zone. Tourism platforms, incorporating three levels: government, business and non-profit organizations, will accelerate regional tourism integration. The platforms at government level should cover policy making, policy support and resourcing. Those at business level should include tourism operation networks and transportation. The non-profit organization platforms should engage in R&D and consultation.

The core concept of creative tourism is building new markets and generating new value. Creative tourism needs to avoid the mistake of relying on heavy investment. Instead we need to enter the 'Blue Ocean' by building the value chain. 'Soft power' will be enhanced at the top end of the tourism value chain through intensive inputs of 'intelligence,' through enhanced integration and the transformation of existing natural, economic and social resources of cities and regions, and through the fostering of new industrial forms of tourism.

Shaolin Culture and Innovation in the Performing Arts

With a history of over 1,500 years the Shaolin Monastery in the Songshan Mountains in Henan Province is the ancestral home of Chan, the largest sect of Chinese Buddhism. It is also the birthplace of the celebrated Shaolin Kung Fu. Shaolin culture, which includes Zen, kung fu, medicine and the arts, has become an international symbol of traditional Chinese culture. The *Zen Shaolin Music Ceremony*, a performing arts event staged in the natural environment of Songshan Mountain has showcased and interpreted Zen culture and Shaolin Kung Fu through the universal languages of music and dance. Exploiting Shaolin's popularity, the show combines the local culture with the unique natural landscape. The performance turns the cultural resources of Shaolin Temple into cultural capital, forming a new identity for Shaolin culture and making significant contributions to local tourism, employment and economic development.

Creative tourism emphasizes the integration and utilization of social resources; it transforms tangible resources (the Songshan landscape, local customs and catering facilities) and intangible resources (Zen religion, Shaolin

Kung Fu, music, and performing arts) into capital. In this way the resources advantage is turned into economic advantage and eventually into cultural brands that will be further invested into tourism industries, stimulating all the links of the industrial value chain and making sustainable contributions to the economy. The resources of Shaolin culture can be transformed through investment, planning, media marketing, and the utilization of natural landscapes.

For creative tourism, the key to wealth creation is to expand the tourism industrial chain. Large numbers of tourists watch the performance show at night and they need to eat, live, get around, and shop. The longer they stay, the more products and services they consume. Since the show was first staged, economic contributions by local hotels and restaurants have increased by 30–40 per cent. The recreational and entertainment facilities built to support the performance, such as Zen Street, the Zen Farm and the Zen Courtyard, have provided the complimentary services of dining, lodging and shopping, extending the tourism industry chain and promoting related local industries including real estate, hotels, restaurants, transportation and services. Through strategic marketing and business operations, the Shaolin Temple and Shaolin culture has turned from a cultural brand to an industry brand, a 'cultural gold mine.' Through various forms of interpretation and the input of modern elements, the core value of the Shaolin culture – Zen religion and martial arts – has been continuously rediscovered, explored, packaged, marketed and utilized.

Creative Agriculture

In the age of creative economy, the construction of a sustainable, healthy rural industrial system through the development of creative agriculture and the transformation of agricultural development is an innovative way to achieve the goals of constructing a new socialist countryside. So-called 'creative agriculture' is not limited to the production of a few agricultural products; it also refers to innovation in the agricultural development model. In comparison with the current development model of 'R&D, production, processing and marketing,' the development model of creative agriculture is characterized by the ability to construct a multi-level, panoramic industrial chain. It will combine cultural and arts activities, agricultural technology, agricultural products, farming activities and market demand to form an interactive industrial value chain.

This will open up new opportunities for the development of agriculture and the development of the countryside. This will also maximize industrial values.

In renovating the development model of agriculture, creative agriculture shifts focus onto the construction of a multi-level industrial chain and value system.

For instance, when we use biotechnology to change the physical functions of agricultural products such as their shape, colour and taste, we can also add cultural value. To meet market demand, we can also utilize creativity to turn agricultural products into art works by designing 'original works from the soil.' This will greatly increase the value added of agricultural products. For example, a basket of small pumpkins, eggplants and zucchinis of various colours and shapes produced by the Shanghai Fengxian Creative Agricultural Park can fetch more than RMB 300. Square-shaped watermelons carrying laser imprints of Olympic images produced by Taiwan farmers have sold for TWD2, 000 each. A pair of walnuts from Beijing, which are named 'lion heads' because of their appearance, have a marked price of RMB 18,000 yuan. Other examples include pictures of classic themes of plants and flowers made of straw, tour maps of the Great Wall made from a variety of peas and portraits of the four legendary ancient beauties in Chinese history made of butterfly wings. The raw materials are not valuable in themselves, but they can become bestselling products of great value after being creatively processed by farmers or being worked with by artists.

Developing creative agriculture means activating cultural resources with the power of storytelling and then transforming these into forms of capital that can bring value added for agriculture. A good case in study is Dalian where corn seeds are planted according to a special labyrinth design which eventually grows into a maze of corn. Coupled with restaurants and other tourist attractions that provide authentic local farmers' meals and showcase farming activities, the labyrinth of corn, the biggest in China, has attracted large numbers of tourists and created new value. China is rich in terms of historical and cultural resources and there are opportunities to make use of these resources to add value to the variety of agricultural products and farming activities through the power of storytelling.

In addition various kinds of festival activities, ceremonial events and production activities attract consumers. Examples include the peach blossoms festival of Nanhui, Shanghai, the bayberries festival of Yuyao, Zhejiang

Province, and the sunflowers festival of Fengle Farm, Henan Province. A variety of cultural performances are orchestrated and presented at these festivals, not only increasing the value of agricultural products and attracting large numbers of tourists but also resulting in the sale of many agricultural products.

For creative agriculture, an industrial grouping consisting of core industries, supporting industries, related industries and merchandising industries can be configured centring on featured products and agricultural zones. In this creative agriculture system primary, secondary and tertiary industries integrate and interact with each other. Furthermore traditional and modern industries, as well as culture and technology will converge. The multiplier effect of industrial value is very obvious here. Currently, Beijing, Shanghai and Guangdong are advocating the development of creative agriculture, but their current practices are limited to the development of featured agricultural products and improved variety of seeds or the development of sightseeing agriculture. Cultural elements need to be added to these projects to improve the industrial chain for the configuration of a large industrial system of creative agriculture.

The development model of creative agriculture not only reflects the requirements of building an economic and ecological civilization but also promotes the development of natural, cultural and social ecology. It has the capacity to construct an ecological civilization characterized by the 'trinity' of natural, cultural and social ecology. For instance, agricultural products can be produced through combining with local natural, cultural and social resources. These products and cultural activities, in which farmers are the key players, not only reflect the productivity of agriculture and the leisure function of culture but also increase famers' income and educational level as well as promote local cultural heritage. In addition, these products and activities restore local social ecology and expand social functions by providing an aesthetic experience of a real, vivid and fresh farming life. The flow of people and money they attract in turn increases the quality of life of farmers and contributes to the creation of vibrant rural communities. As a result, a virtuous cycle of 'snowballing' is created. For example, the Malu Vineyard of Jiading, Shanghai combines tourism, leisure and entertainment services for tourists. People can plant, pick and taste grapes in the vineyard where a fruit and vegetable garden, equipped with modern agricultural facilities and superior variety of seeds, can also help farmers to develop a courtyard economy and to make rural life beautiful to enjoy.

5

The Creative City

Urban Revitalization

In 2004, Tianzifang, a spontaneously initiated creative cluster in the centre of Shanghai, attracted media attention and triggered controversy. *The People's Daily* even published a special report on whether or not Tianzifang should stay or be removed. Some felt it was a cheap restoration of abandoned old factories and warehouses, arguing that it would be more profitable to use Tianzifang for real estate development given that it is conveniently situated on Taikang Road in the centre of Shanghai.

Much of the controversy was due to a lack of understanding of creative industries. While relatively small in size, Tianzifang's seven hectares symbolize high architectural values: namely, an assortment of country-style residences typical of housing south of the Yangzi River, Western colonial style buildings, traditional tenements found only in Shanghai, alleyway buildings and industrial factory buildings built in the 1970s. The diversity of this architecture embodies Shanghai's social and economic development. Indeed, the current clustering of foreign and domestic enterprises in this area has awakened memories of the culture of Shanghai. The Luwan district government has designated the Taikang Road area as a milieu for creative industries rather than for business or real estate development. After several years of government initiatives and industry development, Tianzifang is a success story of urban revitalization; it exemplifies the development track of many modern cities: from efficient cities to creative cities.

Creativity concentrates and thrives in abandoned factories and warehouses in big cities across the world, in turn revitalizing regional economies. The world renowned SOHO district in New York is one of the earliest artists' clusters. It was an industrial district of New York before World War II. The declining manufacturing industry after the war left behind many vacant factory buildings and warehouses. A number of artists renovated them into venues for the production, exhibition and marketing of art. The New York

City government once attempted to demolish all the old buildings to build modern office buildings and luxurious apartment buildings. But this plan was rejected by the public. In the 1970s, the city government eventually decided to categorize SOHO as art-oriented historical and cultural reserve area. Since then, SOHO has flourished.

The site now occupied by London's prestigious Tate Modern was a thermal power plant earmarked for demolition. After redevelopment, the Tate Modern has become a model for Britain's creative industries as well as an art museum that attracts many thousands of visitors. It has helped the region south of the Thames to develop from a poor industrial area into a prosperous cultural centre. Similar cultural revitalization projects include the Hake Xin District of Berlin, the Lan Kwai Island of Vancouver and the Otaru Canal of Hokkaido.

Why then do so many creative activities cluster in old factory buildings and warehouses? Certainly, cheap rent and central location are key attractions. But an important factor is the old buildings with exposed beam structures, which stimulate memory and imagination. Furthermore, the buildings are often wide and spacious, making them easy to re-fit for their new purpose. The environment and atmosphere provided by old factory and warehouse buildings inspires imagination and creative ideas. New ideas arise from the process of exchange, learning and integration of different cultures. In short, artists naturally congregate.

Instead of exhausting increasingly precious natural resources, creative industries protect existing cultural resources; the interaction between artists and urban revitalization helps maintain historical and cultural heritage. Many creative entrepreneurs are young and have few financial resources. So it is natural for these young people to take to the abandoned old city districts to start-up their businesses. In so doing, they have brought new life to the old districts by transforming them into creative spaces.

When manufacturing industries exit the central districts of a city, they leave behind space and industrial infrastructure. How the relevant authorities deal with these resources has an impact on the transformation of urban space. One approach, very common in the new round of rapid development of many Chinese cities, is to demolish buildings and build new ones for other purposes. The problem with this approach is that it is destructive to the cultural ecology and history of a city. Although the city may look better in terms of its appearance, the cultural context is lost in the demolition.

The combination of creative precincts and old city districts can avoid the problem of cultural degradation in cities. Revitalization is not simply about retaining historical infrastructure; in combining past and future, traditional and modern, Eastern and Western, and classic and popular revitalization adds cultural features and stimulates the urban economy. From an economic perspective this approach has the advantage of low cost and high value added. To maintain a selected number of historical buildings representative of industrial society and to leave space for the further development of cultural and creative industries is a positive development concept.

The Cultural Context of the City

Culture contributes to a city's competitive advantage. It provides uniqueness, personality and charm. Without the Palace Museum and *siheyuan*, a historical type of courtyard residence surrounded by four residential buildings, Beijing would have had difficulty getting listed as a city of ancient civilization. Urbanization, characterized by renovation projects in old and structurally dangerous buildings, is driving historical and cultural heritage to disappear. Some cities demolish old buildings and construct replicas. But ancient buildings cannot be reproduced. Even the most exquisite reproductions are considered fakes. This kind of reproduction only serves to diminish a city's cultural context and image.

Urban development should not be at the cost of history. The development of creative industries should be combined with the revitalization of cities as well as the protection of historical and cultural heritage so as to make every building, every street and even the whole city a piece of art, and a cultural product. Tianzifang has maintained the historical and cultural features of more than twenty kinds of tenement in Shanghai. You can find both old and new alleyways lined with buildings featuring architectural styles that include eclecticism, New England renaissance, modernism, traditional Chinese timber and brick, Spanish, British castle and Baroque architecture. But the main feature is the tenement architecture. When planning this cultural and creative industries cluster, the Luwan District government paid special attention to the preservation of the historical appearance and the original architectural styles. Modern elements were added to the redesign and renovation. The finished product has attracted a large number of creative institutions in various industry sectors including architectural design, jewellery design, animation, design, original oil painting, Thai stone carving, folk crafts of Shanxi, Japanese fashion design, collections of Tibetan thangka and the tea ceremony. The cultural context of Shanghai has been extended and developed. Take a walk in the alleys and streets in Tianzifang and you will feel the prosperity of an international metropolis, the richness of Shanghai culture and the vitality of the modern age.

The City Brand

Brand building is usually associated with a business enterprise or a commodity. But a city has a brand and this can be shared by all its businesses and residents. Creativity plays a key role in shaping a city's cultural atmosphere and city branding. It can also help improve the quality of urban life. Ashworth and Voogd believe that creative industries play the role of 'regional marketing'[1] by integrating diverse elements and promoting the character of the city.

Three measures need to be taken to build creative city brands in China. First, there is a need to enhance the links between regions and cities and the collaborative role of creative clusters. By taking advantage of human resources, geographical positioning and investment we can construct regional creative clusters that allow complementary development.

Second, we can improve city competitiveness. The city brand represents the experience and evaluation of the city by consumers, tourists, businessmen, residents and investors. A good city brand produces and maintains reputation and the competitive advantage of the city.

Third, we need to promote urban culture. Culture is the soul of a city. The city brand can have enduring vitality if it accumulates and releases intangible urban assets. Cultural creativity serves as an important means of building a city's core competiveness. Through planning and integration of resources, the city's image can be fostered and intangible assets increased.

[1] Ashworth, G.J. and Voogd, H. (1994), 'Marketing and place promotion', in Gold, J.R. and Ward, S.V. (Eds), *Place Promotion: The Use of Publicity and Marketing to Sell Towns and Regions* (John Wiley & Sons Ltd, Chichester, pp. 39–52).

The Structure of Urban Space

Creative industries optimize the 'centre – periphery' spatial layout of a city through two approaches. One approach accords prominence to the Central Business District (CBD) as the locus of culture and art, a concentration of large museums, opera houses, ballet theatres, movie theatres, libraries and concert halls. An alternative approach is to generate cultural atmosphere by gathering various kinds of creative activities in different urban and suburban districts.

Creative clusters can have positive impacts on the structural layout of urban space. Structure impacts on function. The structural layout of urban space impacts upon how a city functions, how its personality is represented, and the concentration of city industries. On the other hand, highly concentrated and efficient industry clusters optimize the spatial layout of the city.

Richard Florida, Michael Porter – and many Chinese scholars – have studied clusters from regional development and industrial economics perspectives. They believe that creative clusters have a positive impact on the continuation of a city's history and culture and on social transformation.

Some researchers who study urban creative clusters believe that creative clusters have actually become the business card of the city. Examples include art in Florence and the audio-visual products of Wellington, New Zealand.

Some creative clusters function from the standpoint of community. They are the small 'cells' in the city's spatial layout but serve as important bearers of cultural meaning. Often closely related to the lives of city residents, such clusters include museum areas in England, particularly the South Bank in London and the Century Plaza in Birmingham, the Tilburg 013 Music Centre and the performing arts at the Utrecht Theatre Square in the Netherlands, the art design for the old Nokia cable factory in Helsinki, Finland, and Irish pubs in Dublin's Temple District.

Creative clusters' impact on the structural layout of urban space has much to do with their lifecycle. As indicated in Table 5.1, creative clusters, like any other industrial clusters, have a lifecycle that goes through the stages of parasitic – development – thriving – mature. They take on different forms at different stages. At the 'parasitic' stage, creative clusters need public investment in infrastructure. But with continuous growth, these clusters enjoy a more open and mature market that brings about exchange and integration between the city and its neighbouring regions and even between countries. From the micro

Table 5.1 The Evolution of Creative Clusters

Evolutionary Process	Context and Cases
'Parasitic'	Supported by government policy and funding, a number of creative enterprises have been able to develop. Government support includes investment in infrastructure for cultural consumption, convenience for SMEs to raise money, and special allowance for sustainable development of creative clusters.
Examples	• Creative clusters in Britain, such as the Sheffield Cultural Industries Quarter • The Cultural Industries Development Centre in St. Petersburg • The Digital Media City (supported by the Seoul government of South Korea) • Taipei Creative Industries Development • Other developing countries and regions such as the Asia-Pacific region and South America
Development	A number of independent creative enterprises have appeared, together with some privatized cultural enterprises that used to be funded by government. These enterprises are small in scale. The local market for creative enterprises is not fully developed and cultural infrastructure is not complete. There are still traces of government initiatives.
Examples	• Creative clusters in Brisbane • Music communities in Tilburg • The (proposed) West Kowloon Cultural District in Hong Kong
Thriving	Thanks to increased government investment in cultural infrastructure, creative enterprises have increased in number and in scale. Local and regional markets have expanded and begun to reach consumers in international markets.
Examples	• Product design, architecture, digital media in Barcelona • Film and TV in Glasgow

Mature	In some industries, large-scale creative enterprises have become the dominant force of clusters. They have highly developed domestic and international markets and carry out sophisticated sub-outsourcing business.
Examples	• Film and TV clusters in Los Angeles • Fashion and furniture design in Milan • Fashion in New York

Source: Strategies for Creative Spaces, www.creativelondon.org.uk

level, creative clusters start to gradually impact on and actually change the spatial structure of cities.

Creative Clusters

While there are different categorizations of creative clusters in the research literature, I identify three types in respect to impetus and function: first, those that are organically formed and are driven by aesthetic creativity; second, those that largely generate economic value; and third, those that embody social and historical significance. In the following section I will provide examples of creative clusters, and particularly creative clusters in China.

Activating artistic inspirations: organic space driven by creativity

Gathered in this typology we find mostly non-profit art organizations. The Singapore artists' village in north-western Sembawang is an independent collective formed in 1988; it is relatively isolated with minimum outside disturbance. It extends from village space to urban houses and urban offices or art design areas. Artists are the 'impetus' for this type of creative cluster. The space is based on 'organic organization' and 'live order.' As an organic process of social organization, it is replacing space based on mechanical organization. Because it is non-profit, artists' activities are not limited to studios or galleries. They rely more on public venues to do their creative work. These venues include residential houses, trade spaces, parks, cultural sites, galleries and art colleges.

This type of cluster is promoted by art groups and social groups, rather than business groups. It places more emphasis on artists' inspirations and the artistic pursuit of the cluster as a whole than on profit making. Clusters under this category often emerge spontaneously in international cities. Though small in scale, they flourish rapidly thanks to innovative milieus. The innovative environment includes diversified cultural patterns, a good IP protection system, a long-term talent strategy and tolerance of bohemian and pioneer cultural formations.

Songzhuang is a village in the outer eastern suburbs of Beijing. Ever since 1993, artists have been coming to Songzhuang and nearby villages to set up their own studios, workshops and galleries. In recent years there has been an increase in the migration of artists to Songzhuang and it has earned a reputation as a contemporary artist village; the majority of artists rent abandoned industrial buildings and residential houses. Many have built elaborate studios and workspaces. The architectural styles of the village are now very different from before, illustrating the integration of artists into the population. After eighteen years of development, Songzhuang is the biggest cluster of original artists in China; there are more than 3,000 artists in various fields, such as painting, sculpture, music, literature, film and television. Songzhuang has transformed from a residential area for artists into a cluster where artists, galleries, critics and agents concentrate. Its widespread reputation as an art cluster can be compared to that of Paris' Barbizon district, New York's SOHO, and Germany's Dachau and Worpswede.

While Songzhuang is a spontaneously-formed creative cluster, the important point to note is that its success has promoted the development of related industries. Art has provided the impetus. Songzhuang has the necessary elements of a creative cluster; it provides infrastructure, public services, residential and consumption environments: moreover, it has a certain industrial scale and independent R&D capacity; it has specialized service institutions and public service platforms. Artists and freelancers display products that are often original and experimental. They have an acute sense of the market and are engaged in business activities in relation to art products. As a result, Songzhuang has rapidly become a primary market for art production and has stimulated the development of a local art trade and related industries.

M50 (50 Moganshan Road) is one of Shanghai's most influential art centres with 130 artists and artist organizations from within China, and from over twenty countries and regions, on site. M50 was referred to by *Time* magazine as 'the fashion landmark of Shanghai'. The way M50 was formed is in fact similar to New York's SOHO and Beijing's 798. Established in 2000, M50 has kept intact the unique factory buildings of China's national textile industry built between the 1930s and the 1990s. In the late 1990s, the textile enterprises started to move out of the city as a result of Shanghai's move to readjust its industrial structure. The abandoned factory buildings were put up for rent. Attracted by cheap rent, artists moved to Morganshan Road. That was the humble beginnings of M50, one of the earliest clusters in Shanghai. Today, the clustering effect has enabled M50 to expand from an artist precinct to a creative cluster that involves a variety of sectors. It has established a complete industrial chain as well as an operating model in which similar industries concentrate, and in which different industries complement each other.

Importantly, the relationship between industries is more complementary than competitive. For example, the M50 Alliance, a loose concentration of institutions and artists, is able to use M50's brand value for external tender. The Alliance has successfully landed a large contract for a large-scale comprehensive planning project, which could not be achieved by any individual artist. Artists are collaborative and competitive, which is healthy for the development of production and business networks. Both individual artist and the Alliance can engage in design, production and marketing. This has helped produce a culture that has brought profits for M50. On the other hand, M50 is taking the initiative to invest in infrastructure to attract more creative people. It has a plan in place to build, beyond an industrial cluster, an 'art community' that will 'combine work and life' as lifestyle.

Creating economic value: enterprise clusters that focus on cost

The natural agglomeration of enterprises represents another creative cluster model, the original purpose of which is often to reduce costs for participating enterprise. A typical example is Hollywood, which was initially formed as a spontaneous concentration of small and medium-sized enterprises. 'Localized external economies' identified by the neoclassical economist Alfred Marshall are produced here; namely specialized suppliers and labour markets. The final product is provided by film studios or TV networks. But it is actually the final result of a complex network that involves independent producers, actors and actresses, agents, legal advisers and special effects technicians. These people come from different professions and use different facilities in their pursuit of professional perfection. No individual company alone can cater to this huge demand. Bringing it all together in one place became the best solution for the movie and TV industries in America. In the beginning, small and medium-sized companies came to Hollywood; individually they could not afford the infrastructure of transport, studios and outdoor locations. The concentration of film production bases, film processing plants, post-production companies and distribution companies reduced the shooting time of a film as well as crew costs. In addition, soft infrastructure such as film systems and regulations established through continuous collaboration and competition among enterprises further facilitated the growth of those companies. The prosperity of Hollywood has in turn attracted skilled people from all over the world; their participation has helped to promote Hollywood and its globalization.

The last type of cluster features large cultural institutions or business groups. These core organizations are surrounded by a large number of smaller elements leading to overall economies of scale. The Hengdian Film and TV Group, located in Zhejiang is an example. It has invested an accumulated RMB three billion in construction and has established a competitive market based around its low cost production system. By 2011, it had built thirteen film and TV sets and two super large modern studios. Engaged in the shooting, production and distribution of films and TV drama serials, the Hengdian Group has gradually extended its activities into film and TV exhibition, research, and entertainment and film tourism.

Social attributes: urban cultural districts with historical significance

The third type of cluster refers to urban areas that attract social and cultural capital. These clusters include city buildings, educational institutions, religious temples and cultural buildings, which are often architecturally and historically significant and are intended as gathering places for a range of activities.

Shanghai has a large number of old industrial buildings that have witnessed not only Shanghai's history of industrial society but also China's industrial history. In recent years, many have been abandoned due to urban transformation. But the city government has set up an initiative to protect industrial, historical and cultural heritage by attracting foreign or local business capital. The historical and cultural contexts remain intact and the imaginative space unique to old industrial buildings can be interpreted and expanded. These buildings have become unique resources. With old building-based clusters accounting for two thirds of the city's total creative clusters, this type of cluster has become the main characteristic of Shanghai. Representative of this type of cluster are 1933 Old Millfun that used to be a slaughterhouse, Bridge 8 which was transformed from old workshops of an automotive brakes factory, and Tianzifang featuring old tenement buildings unique to Shanghai.

Another relevant example is 2577 Creative Compound in the Xuhui District of Shanghai. Formerly the base for the Jiangnan Manufacturing Bureau, the first headquarters of China's modern industry, it later accommodated China's first institute of industrial design. Today, it has been transformed into offices championing an ecological environment of low density, low volume and landscaped gardens. It combines multiple functions including office space, exhibition, product release, leisure and sightseeing. It has turned the cultural and historical elements of old factory buildings into an inspiration, a combination of culture, history, creativity and art.

There is no strict demarcation between the three types of creative clusters, of course. Those organic spaces created by artists' inspirations may give way to other kinds of development if increased rent forces non-profit institutions to move out. And some cultural places and public space, such as popular city parks and special cultural buildings may attract the attention of artists' and become their extended space of artistic creation.

Beijing's Songzhuang, Shanghai's M50 and 2577 Creative Compound concentrate cultural spirit and carry the historical and future missions of the city. They have given new life to old buildings and new charm to a city by integrating cultural creativity into urban planning and by creating a new cultural environment. Shanghai is becoming more attractive as a creative city because of the existence of many M50s and 2577s. And China is more powerfully placed as a rising power because of the many fledgling creative cities. It proves that if creativity can change the fate of individuals and the image of cities, it is also capable of changing, and is in fact changing China.

With increasing globalization and international competition in today's world, creative industries are not simply a development concept. World-class cities, such as London, New York, Paris and Tokyo, have been revitalized. In China, the positive impact of the creative industries on cities is yet to be fully realized.

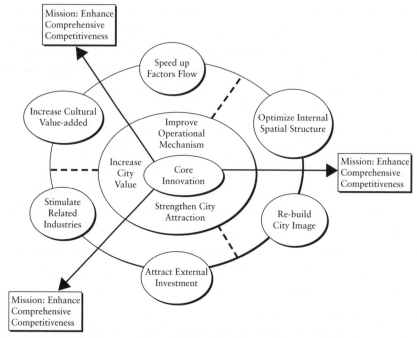

Figure 5.1 The Roadmap to Strengthening City Competitiveness through Innovation

Opportunities for Creative Industries in Urban Transformation

These changes in urban development have provided huge opportunities which can be summarized as following:

First, due to the continuous increase of urban land and labour costs, there are changes in the driving forces of economic growth. According to American economist Michael Porter, economic growth was first driven by resources and then by investment. But when the marginal benefit of investment starts to decline, innovation becomes the driving force of economic growth. Since innovation includes scientific innovation and cultural innovation, creative industries, combining cultural creativity and high technology, are the best choice for urban economic development.

Second, rising economic levels have led to changes in consumption patterns with people demanding more cultural products once material needs are satisfied. Well-known American futurist John Naisbitt once said that in modern society, people are more eager to look for the meaning of life than daily necessities and security; they are in pursuit of something abstract that is higher, deeper and more far-reaching. One of the things creative industries can do is provide rich cultural products to satisfy people's growing and increasingly urgent need for culture. In this sense, cities have provided a huge market for creative industries.

Third, constrained by resources and the environment, cities need sustainable development. The concept of creative industries itself was developed from the attempt by old industrial cities to overcome the problems of high energy consumption, high pollution and low value added of manufacturing industries. Urban development, increasing business costs and continuous adjustment of urban industrial structure have forced industries out of urban areas. And due to limited land resources, metropolitan cities can no longer allow the development of low-end manufacturing industries. Those high value-added manufacturing industries and service industries are given high priority instead, which provides a development space for creative activities. When we are constrained by material and natural resources, we need to develop intangible resources. This plays a very important role in reducing pollution and achieving sustainable development.

Finally, scientific and technological development has expanded the development space for creative industries. The rapid development of science and technology has to some degree impacted on traditional cultural industries but has enabled creative industries to get strong, multidimensional technological support. Science and technology have created many new art forms and opened up new fields for creative industries. Information technology has created the preconditions for the development of creative industries by creating virtual spaces and changing how urban residents consume, communicate and participate in activities. The internet and digital technology have extended the industrial chain of creative industries by expanding and promoting industry convergence; boundaries between industries have become blurred.

Promotion of Sustainable Development of the Urban Economy

Creative industries are gradually replacing the manufacturing industries that consume resources and pollute the environment. They expand the economic ties of a city and enhance the service functions of regional centres. In cities that have weak natural resources creative industries can promote modern service industries. Creative industries with local characteristics can be developed to produce high-tech, high cultural content and high value-added products and services. By taking advantage of cultural creativity to make up for disadvantage in resources and capital, creative industries can provide new impetus for sustainable economic development.

Creativity in China

International metropolises are places where creative industries are most highly developed. Creative industries and creative cities are like twins growing up together. Creative cities are nourished by creative industries while creative industries flourish in the appropriate environment provided by the creative cities. Since 2004 when China's Creative Industries Forum was held, Beijing, Shenzhen, Shanghai and some other Chinese cities have been bent on developing creative industries in their drive to achieve the strategic target of becoming 'creative cities.' Different cities have different approaches, taking into account their own strength and advantages.

Beijing

As the political centre of China and a centre of international cultural exchange, Beijing has many advantages. It has exceptionally rich cultural resources; its cultural atmosphere attracts skills, technology and advanced management concepts and ideas. It has the largest number of creative workers (more than 960,000) of all Chinese cities.[2] In 2009 when the Chinese economy was experiencing difficulties due to the global recession, Beijing's cultural and creative industries achieved RMB 149.77 billion in value added, accounting for 12.6 per cent of the city's GDP. The output value of its cultural content industries accounted for over 40 per cent of the national total.[3] The output value of its animation and online games alone was more than RMB 8 billion in 2009, accounting for one quarter of the national total. Statistics from the first three quarters of 2009 show that of the nine sectors of cultural and creative

---

[2] Jincheng Zhang. *Chinese Creative Industries Report (2009)*, Beijing: Chinese Economic Publication House, 2009.
[3] Analysis on Beijing Cultural Creative Industries Development. http://www.askci.com/freereports/2010-01/201012795324.html [accessed 8 March 2011].

industries, software, computer network and computer serv.
and exhibition, news and publishing, and radio and television w.
performers in terms of added value. In 2006, Beijing's municipal gove.
established a special fund of RMB 500 million per year for the development
cultural and creative industries. Since then, RMB 2 billion has been allocated
to support 365 key projects in promoting cultural and creative industries while
investment capital of nearly RMB 20 billion has been raised.[4]

Currently, Beijing's creative industries have six major centres: the national
art performance centre, the national publishing and copyright trade centre,
the national film and TV program production and trading centre, the national
animation and internet games development and production centre, the national
cultural convention centre, and the national trading centre for antique art. As
the capital of China, Beijing enjoys an advantage of unique competitiveness
over other Chinese cities in terms of government support. For example, the
Beijing International Cultural and Creative Industries Expo was supported by
various ministries and departments of the central government. Beijing is also
quick in implementing its cultural soft power strategy, which can be seen in the
continuous expansion of development plans for cultural and creative clusters
such as the Green International Port of Shunyi, the Huairou film production
base and the Songzhuang art cluster.

Shanghai

Shanghai is the most economically developed city in China. Shanghai culture,
a fusion of Eastern and Western cultures features tolerance, innovation and
business and provides a good cultural atmosphere and rich resources for
creative industries. In terms of investment and financing, Shanghai attracts
most international capital. Since 2005 when Shanghai's first Creative Industries
Week was held, Shanghai has become the forerunner of China's cultural and
creative industries. By the end of 2009, there were eighty-one established
creative clusters in Shanghai with 4,000 enterprises in residence and 80,000
employees. Around RMB 7 billion of business capital had been invested in the
construction of creative clusters. It is expected that there will be 100 clusters

---

[4] The Official document Beijing Policies on Promoting Development of Cultural and Creative
Industries was announced by Beijing Municipal Development and Reform Commission on 6 Nov
2006.

by the end of 2010 and the total output value of creative clusters will be RMB 50 billion by the end of 2012. In 2008, Shanghai's creative industries achieved RMB 104,875 billion in value added with an average annual increase of over 20 per cent, accounting for 7.66 per cent of the city's GDP. Both the industrial scale and the growth rate of creative industries in Shanghai are ahead of other Chinese cities.

Shanghai's approach to creative industries is to transform and upgrade traditional industries and to combine the renovation of old urban districts with the protection of cultural and historical heritage. Currently, the Shanghai Creative Industries Association has more than 200 members. The Shanghai World Expo 2010 was a super engine for Shanghai's creative industries. The goal is to build Shanghai into an 'international centre of creative industries' comparable to London, New York and Tokyo. In 2010, Shanghai was granted the title of City of Design by UNESCO and became the member of UNESCO Creative Cities Network. By taking advantage of its comprehensive advantages in finance, trade and shipping, Shanghai hopes to become a major force in stimulating the development of creative industries in China and throughout the world.

The World Expo 2010 Shanghai

The World Expo 2010 Shanghai provided a rare opportunity for the development of Shanghai's creative industries. The Expo inspired innovation through the exchange of scientific and cultural ideas and achievements from different countries and regions. The emblem and mascot of the World Expo Shanghai as well as the master plan and the design of major venues were based on designs from all over the world. The collection of these designs was actually a process of multicultural exchange; different countries' ideas became sources of inspiration.

The World Expo 2010 Shanghai greatly promoted the development of sectors such as advertising, architectural design, fashion design, film and broadcasting, publishing, the performing arts, music and computer software services. Moreover, many of the Expo venues have become creative clusters and are expected to attract more creative people, which will help Shanghai to become a true international centre of cultural exchange. Finally, the Expo has pushed Shanghai's IP protection to a new level and this will help regulate and protect the sustainable development of Shanghai's cultural and creative industries.

The World Expo 2010 Shanghai also provided a big opportunity for the Yangzi Delta area. The diffusion effects of the Expo have assisted economic integration in the Yangzi Delta. After Shanghai's successful bid for the World Expo, business enterprises in neighbouring Jiangsu province and Zhejiang province began to use the World Expo brand. Now they are taking advantage of the World Expo 2010 Shanghai to showcase their economic, cultural and scientific achievements.

Shenzhen

In December of 2008, Shenzhen became an official 'City of Design' when UNESCO approved its application. It became the sixteenth member of the global creative city network. Shenzhen is the first Chinese city to be accepted into this global network. It has advantages in terms of export networks in toy design, software design, industrial design and architectural design. It has 60 per cent of the domestic market in industrial design. Its creative industries are mainly design-related such as printing, animation, architecture and fashion. One of Shenzhen's well-known creative industries clusters is the Dafen Oil Painting Village, known as 'China's No. 1 oil painting village,' the products of which are sold mainly to European, American and African buyers. China (Shenzhen) International Cultural Industries Fair serves to further promote Shenzhen's creative economy. Taking advantage of the international stage provided by being a global 'capital of design,' Shenzhen has combined brand management with product design in order to transform from selling products to selling design, from material products to design products and from a processing base to a design base. This approach is also providing new impetus for creative industries.

The Shenzhen Municipal government has provided generous support for its cultural and creative industries ever since 2004 when the city established the objectives of building a 'capital of creative design.' The government support includes a number of policy documents, a special fund of RMB 300 million each year for cultural industries in the forms of loan interest subsidies and incentives, a three-year exemption from corporate income tax for cultural start-ups, and the annual 'Creative December' activity that calls for new ideas for developing cultural and creative industries. In 2007, Shenzhen issued the 'Shenzhen Declaration' to further promote creative industries and included cultural and creative industries into its 11th five-year plan for economic and social development. The rapid development of Shenzhen's creative industries has attracted international design skills, capital, exhibitions, and creative enterprises. It has also helped Shenzhen's creative design to serve the whole country and to go to the world. It is helping Shenzhen's enterprises to transform from 'Made in Shenzhen' to 'Created in Shenzhen.'

Hangzhou

Hangzhou achieved per capita GDP of US$10,968 in 2009. After hosting the World Leisure Expo 2006 and the China Creative Industries Expo in 2007, Hangzhou has established leisure industries as its economic growth point and has built five kinds of recreational venues including leisure and holiday, entertainment, sports and fitness, dining, and shopping. Representative of Hangzhou's creative clusters are A8 Art Tribe, 433 Tang Shang, LOFT 49 and Baimahu (White Horse Lake) Eco-village. These creative clusters have the distinctive features of the post-industrial era. Following the lead of LOFT 49, the 'West Lake Creative Alley' and Zhejiang's first creative industries experimental zone was established. Under the city's development strategy of 'one city, seven centres,' Hangzhou is focused on developing cultural and creative industries into the city's new leading industries within three years. Taking advantages of its competitiveness in talent, environment, market, industry and culture, Hangzhou expects to become a world-class national centre of cultural and creative industries.

Guangzhou

Due to proximity to Hong Kong and being one of the pioneers in China's opening up and reform, Guangzhou was the first Chinese city to see a concentration of advertising, film and TV, media and IT networks. In 2009, Guangzhou achieved RMB 900 billion in GDP and over US$10,000 in per capita GDP, retaining its third-place position among other Chinese cities. However, there is still much to improve in the municipal government's approach to creative industries and the making and implementing of related policies. The 11th Five-year Plan indicates that Guangzhou has designated a number of areas for the construction of creative parks such as the Lutheran International Centre at the 'Creative South Bay,' the Guangzhou Design Port at Liwan and the Tianhe Online Games and Animation Industrial Base.

Chengdu

Chengdu has the double resources of creativity and vitality. No online games developer can afford to ignore Chengdu which is one of the leading top three cities in the digital entertainment industry in China, followed by Beijing and Shanghai. The city has intangible cultural heritage (such as the Jinsha Site) and traditional cultural resources (such as the cultural heritage of Romance of Three Kingdoms, a classic of Chinese literature). With a view to becoming China's leading city in original animation, the municipal government has established the target of building 'two centres and four 100[5]' to strengthen its R&D in digital entertainment. The city's first cultural and creative industries park, the Red Star Road 35, was established in September of 2007. It is regarded as the beginning of Chengdu's creative industries and is expected to become Chengdu's 798.

Chongqing

China's Creative Industries Forum was first opened in Chongqing in January, 2005. The following year saw the establishment of a special task group and an office by the municipal government to promote creative industries. In June, 2007, the first batch of nine designated creative industries demonstration bases was established. The Huangjueping Graffiti Art Street became the longest designated street for graffiti art in China at 1.25 kilometres. In the same year, Chongqing held its first Creative Industries Week at which, products of modern art, architectural design, creative advertising, arts and crafts, and animation were exhibited. On the other hand, the Sichuan Academy of Fine Arts, an incubator of modern art, reflects the development of Chongqing's creative industries.

Wuhan

Wuhan has the reputation of a city with a large number of institutions of higher learning, giving it a talent advantage for cultural and creative industries. Wuhan

---

[5] Four 100 refers to the goal of Chengdu government initiatives, namely 'To establish 100 digital entertainment R&D centres, to develop 100 products with independent IP rights, to attract over 100 high-end representatives of talent, to reach economic output driven by digital entertainment over 10 billion yuan by 2010 in Chengdu.'

started with animation and has sought to position itself as one of China's key training bases for animators and persons working in animation sectors. In an attempt to build the 'creative centre' of China, the city plans to divide its digital creative industries parks (represented by the Optical Valley) into five areas including the National Animation Industry Park, the National Digital Media Centre, the IC Design Park, and the Industrial Design Industry Park. However, lack of overall planning and lack of investment have contributed to the relative slow development of Wuhan's cultural and creative industries which are still largely in the initial stage.

Xi'an

Xi'an is an ancient city with a rich cultural heritage. It has the fourth largest number of institutions of higher learning in China; its per capita education index is among the highest in China. The film and TV sectors are well represented, numbering more than 200 enterprises and institutions. The output and influence of Xi'an in these sectors is second only to Beijing. Currently, under the banner of 'imperial revival,' Xi'an is striving to build a modern metropolis to showcase the 'new Silk Road' while maintaining the historical legacy of the former capital of four dynasties. Xi'an will be rebuilt into two urban areas (the old and the new) and different approaches will apply. In the renovation of the old urban area, ancient cultural elements will be maintained and regenerated. In the construction of the new urban area, the combination of modern and ancient culture is emphasized. This combined approach will make the two areas showcases of distinctive and unique features, highlighting the relationship between ancient and modern civilization and between cultural and ecological resources.

Nanjing

As a city of rich historical and cultural resources, Nanjing is well equipped to develop creative industries. In 2007, Nanjing's cultural and creative industries generated RMB 30.265 billion in value added, up 18 per cent from the previous year; the contribution to the economy was 9.22 per cent. There are now forty-one cultural industry parks, including Creative East 8 District, Yinkun West Temple Digital Network Cultural Park, Stone Castle Modern Art Creative Park, National Animation Industrial Base at Nanjing High-tech Development

Zone, and four animation industrial incubator bases. They are engaged in cultural and performing arts education, architectural and decorative design, aviation design and the development of high technology, advertising design, and creation and exhibition of art. In 2004, Nanjing successfully hosted the third 'Nanjing Cultural Industry Fair of China' and the 'Nanjing Historical and Cultural Cities Expo of China.' The two cultural platforms not only showcased the rich context and achievements of cultural industries but also attracted investment and business for Nanjing's cultural and creative industries.

Creativity is widely recognized as an economic driving force for wealth creation, employment, sustainable urban development, technological transformation, industrial innovation, and a driver for urban and national competitiveness. In the past few decades, the economic development of cities globally has turned from focusing on ordinary service industries to paying more attention to the ability to innovate in the knowledge-based creative economy. For China, creative industries are a strategic choice to increase urban competitiveness and to achieve sustainable urban development.

6

Towards a Creative Society

As I have shown in the preceding chapters creative industries policy takes various forms and approaches. In China, governments at national as well as regional level have issued policies to support cultural and creative industries despite controversies and contested definitions. The rapid development of creative industries demonstrates that the construction of a creative economy is inevitably coupled with social restructuring and transformation.

The Evolution of Creative Communities

In contrast to industries that are reliant on hard infrastructural factors such as land, machinery and buildings, creative industries develop in response to 'soft' factors including creativity, culture, brands and intellectual property. This soft infrastructure gives rise to 'creative communities,' that is, various groups form with networked social relations and activities. How these 'creative communities' operate ultimately impacts on the sustainability of creative industries.

Many different understandings of creative industries emerge from different disciplines and perspectives. The academic understanding of creative industries has evolved over the past decade. I believe we are seeing three interconnected phases of development in China: I describe these as the *creative industries*, the *creative economy* and the *creative society*. This is illustrated in Table 6.1.

The *creative industries* reflect the contribution that culture and art make to the economy. The *creative economy* demonstrates how creativity is used to stimulate innovation in other economic domains; that is outside the so-called creative industries. The *creative society* illustrates wider spillover effects, for instance, forms of interaction between creative precincts and social groups, the building of communities within creative cities, and eventually the task of making a creative nation.

Table 6.1 The Evolution of Creative Industries

Phase	I. Creative Industries	II. Creative Economy	III. Creative Society
Factor	Culture, Art, Creativity	• Intellectual Property • Symbolic value	• Citizen's right; • Consumer's recognition
Form	• Cultural industry • Creative clusters	• Creativity as intermediate input factors • Build up of creative industrial chain	• Creative city • Creative class • Creative community
Feature	Creative output	Creative input	Creative spillover
Industry	Key industries	Convergent industries	Branding symbol of industries
Target	To promote creative output	To foster innovations in broader domains	To build creative communities
Policy implication	• To improve industry value added • New wealth creation	• To transform the economic development model • Creative industries as part of a system of innovation	• Consumer as input factors • economic & social co-developed structure with people at the centre • to build up enabling creative environment
Policy focus	To nurture the source of creativity	To build up soft creative environment for creative transformation and input	Reconfiguration of consumption, educational system and institutional system

Reform and social transformation are major development goals underwriting creative industries policy. Internationally, creative industries have entered the creative economy phase; indeed, many nations are already at the doorstep of the creative society. Currently, China is evolving from creative industries to the creative economy. In many regions and districts creative enterprises are locked in the industrial phase; furthermore, the values of creativity are yet to significantly influence the structural organization of industries in the broader economy.

The creative industries phase witnessed rapid expansion in a number of industry sectors deemed to produce wealth and employment. The British Labour government's Department for Culture, Media and Sport (DCMS) identified thirteen sectors: advertising, architecture, art and the antiques market, crafts, design, designer fashion, film, interactive and leisure software, music, performing arts, publishing, software development, television and radio.[1] Sectors with information, content and culture as core elements were promoted.

This initial phase was followed by worldwide efforts to brand 'capitals of creativity.' A number of projects have aligned with post-industrial transformation and urban regeneration agendas. New York, for instance, claims a city spirit founded on a 'high degree of integration, excellent creativity, strong competitiveness and extraordinary resilience.' London has identified a clear development target of becoming 'the world's centre of excellence in creativity and culture.' Tokyo meanwhile has launched a development strategy to become a 'cultural city full of creativity'; Singapore is oriented toward 'the creative centre of a new Asia' and 'the global centre of cultural and design industries.' Hong Kong is determined to build into 'an open and diversified international cultural metropolis.'[2]

In *The Creative Economy* John Howkins defined creative industries from the perspective of intellectual property. Howkins argues that copyright, patent, and trademarks conjoin the creative industries and the creative economy.[3] He extended the DCMS definition to include patent-related R&D activities in various fields of the natural sciences. This approach effectively resolves the problem of separating scientific creativity from culture and art. It also shifts

---

[1] *Creative Industries Mapping Document*, issued in November of 1998 by the British Department for Culture, Media and Sport (DCMS).

[2] Li Wuwei's Keynote speech 'Towards City of Creativity' at Shanghai Creative Industries International Forum 2008, Shanghai.

[3] Howkins, John (2001). *The Creative Economy: How people make money from ideas*, UK: Penguin Business.

emphasis from the specific industry level towards the task of upgrading the whole economic system.

The creative economy phase has two distinguishing characteristics. First, creative industries are now regarded as more than just cultural and content industries. They are 'boundary-less':[4] they constitute inputs into other industrial sectors and in so doing they promote the transformation of the economy and models of innovation.[5] The second distinguishing feature is that developing countries have realized the importance of creative industries and have started to enact strategies according to their respective cultural resources.

The creative society phase sees creative industries activities 'breaking out' into a variety of social fields, often beyond the economic frame of reference. A good example is creative clusters. They are no longer just 'precincts' or 'old warehouses' enclosed by walls; they are open communities combining work, life and commercial activities. Tianzifang, the first such creative cluster in Shanghai, experienced a transition from rented 'old factory buildings' in street alleys to street blocks (in terms of space), from single to multiple (in terms of industry form), and from factory to community (in terms of development model). A community-oriented development pattern, linking precinct, business district and the city has taken shape.

The Creative Community

Creative industries are challenging narrow understandings of economy. It may be said that creative industries are 'living industries' in the new economic society. We will further analyse and understand this idea from the perspective of community.

In a broad sense, community refers to social relations in certain regions or fields. It can represent a network of embedded mutual relationships or it can imply designated social relationships. Alternatively, the term 'creative community' reflects a necessary sociality related to the development of creative industries. This term emphasizes social ecology; it gives prominence

[4] Huimin Wang 5C Model: New Development Concept in Tourism Industry. *China Industrial Economy*, 2007, p. 6.
[5] Wuwei Li and Huimin Wang 'Creative Industries: An innovation of development model', *Wenhui Bao*, 12 March 2007.

to the profound impact of creative industries on social organization and social transformation.

The concept of 'creative communities' has been used by John Eger of San Diego State University.[6] This idea was conceived relative to the concept of 'smart communities'.[7] Eger observed that the key to urban development is employment and wealth creation, together with improvement in quality of life. An important task therefore is to reorganize communities so as to accommodate a different kind of society under the knowledge economy. Central to this task is confirming the role of culture and the arts in promoting economic development and establishing a 'creative community', a process in which interactions between culture, art, industry and community are fully exploited, a process in which there is investment in human resources and capital. This prepares the ground for challenges brought about by rapid industrialization and the knowledge-based economy.

The creative community does not necessarily infer a particular geographical environment. Rather, it is a general term referring to 'communities' and social relations. It includes enterprise communities, special interest communities (such as those organized around animation, music and film), and specific class communities (such as the creative class, consumer alliances that have a positive impact on creativity, educators, and those being educated). In the evolution from creative industries to the creative economy and on to the creative society, these communities provide the impetus for sustainable development; they serve as crucial cells; they are the driving engine for the restructuring of social organizations and the transformation of society.

Creative communities can therefore be understood as living cells in the organizational system of creative industries. In this sense they indicate interrelated networks of people connected with the development of creative industries, living communities that form 'socially', and which engage in creative

[6] John Eger, *The Creative Community: Forging the Links Between Art Culture Commerce & Community* (San Diego: California Institute for Smart Communities, SDSU International Center for Communications, 2003). Available: http://www.thecreativecommunity.org/ [accessed 8 March 2011].

[7] A smart community is a community that has made a conscious effort to use information technology to transform life and work within its region in significant and fundamental rather than incremental ways. The goal of such an effort is more than the mere deployment of technology. Rather it is about preparing one's community to meet the challenges of a global, knowledge economy. Available: http://www.smartcommunities.org/concept.php [accessed 8 March 2011].

R&D, production, sales and exchange. Such social relationships facilitate the convergence of culture and art, business, technology and human development in economic development and social progress. In terms of actual form creative communities are represented by a variety of networks, platforms, theme activities or exchange mechanisms. These networks are dynamic, often loose and virtual.

Creative communities engage with most content and activities related to the soft infrastructure of creative clusters, creative classes and creative districts. *Creative clusters* are groupings of manufacturing and business activities consisting largely of creative enterprises. The *creative class* describes groupings of creative talent that generate creative outputs as well as R&D. *Creative districts* are exchange and consumption communities represented in the form of urban space and residents. These three kinds of communities provide the main energy of the creative industries. Their relationships are shown in Figure 6.1.

Unlike physical clusters, class-based groupings and venues located in districts, creative communities are living organisms where innovative activities are inspired and produced.

The creative community has the following features:

- **Organic and interactive:** the creative community is the organic link between specific communities and related production, promotion and consumption of a creative product. This link is neither a one-way and

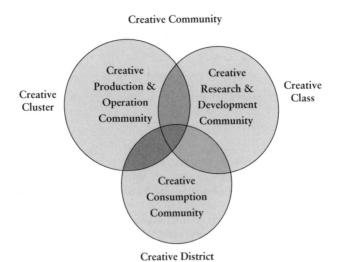

Figure 6.1 The Relations Between Creative Cluster, Creative Class and Creative District

linear connection nor an affiliation or administrative relationship. Rather, it is a process of mutual integration and interaction. One creative community can interact and integrate with different creative clusters, creative classes and creative communities at the same time.

- **A loose network:** People of different ages, races and occupations from anywhere in the world can become members of the same creative community. The organizational structure is typically loose and the networks are mutually-linked. Members have access in order to communicate freely; there are distribution channels for feedback.

- **Various theme activities:** particular interest, projects or incidents are often the initial incentive for the formation of a creative community. For example, the American TV drama series *Prison Break* was a hit in China. A group of fans established the *Prison Break* community in which members created story ideas and designed different endings for the fate of the main character. In a similar way, innovative developers formed the Open Source Code movement and volunteers established the Olympic community. Many groups of sports followers and fans of celebrities and stars have formed their own communities.

The relationship between creative communities and creative industries can be compared to the relationship between the single 'bit' and IT. The creative community is the 'bit' of creative industries; it is both the basic organizational unit and the unique 'DNA.' Different types of creative industries from different regions can be constructed, identified and developed through creative communities. As we know, cultural and social capital constitute human creativity, art and culture. These two forms of capital reflect the fact that creative industries require an appropriate cultural and social ecology for survival, development and growth. Creative communities are basic organizational units in the construction of a sound ecological environment. And because of their close connection with local cultural and social resources, capital and networks, creative communities embody distinct local features and regional characteristics. The creative community is the 'DNA' of creative industries, nourishing growth from regional cultures. The community provides resources for sustainable development of creativity because it is a dynamic source of innovation.

The role of such communities, as living cells in the development of creative industries can be likened to the role of enzymes in the metabolism of living organisms. The capacity to synergize, catalyze and fuse provides sustainability and in this way reshapes a new social structure.

Communities provide synergy; they stimulate capital. Initially they tend to cluster in urban spaces, followed by a gradual reaching out, a process which can generate socio-economic transformations in cities and regions. Organic interaction within and between such communities is advantageous to the agglomeration of resources such as talent, enterprise and capital. Such resource factors improve quality of life for local residents and assist in improving cultural capital. The unique cultural brands generated by creative communities improve the overall value of the region. Regional creative culture has become a source of differential land rent. Tianzifang in Shanghai's Luwan District and Bridge 8 are examples that demonstrate how creative activities and the clustering of key factors have contributed not only to the appreciation of property but also to a rise in local residents' quality of life.

The programming of festivals (e.g. film festivals, art festivals and carnivals) and events (e.g. Olympic Games, World Expo) plays an important role in regional development. Since 1947, when France launched the first Cannes film festival, Cannes has transformed from a small beachfront city to a world-renowned location that attracts large numbers of both business groups and individual tourists. More than 60,000 film professionals and 200,000 tourists attend the Cannes festival each year. Over the eleven days direct income from venue rental, hotels, restaurants, transportation, fashion, general merchandise, tourist souvenirs and camera equipment is 200 million Euros while indirect economic turnover is 700 million Euros. More important however is the fact that Cannes now runs its economy based on trade shows and tourism. Currently, Cannes contributes 300 days a year to various trade shows and exhibitions involving many economic fields including film, TV, mobile phones, motor vehicles, boats, jewellery, IT, tourism and architecture. Cannes becomes the focus of global attention each year at the time of the film festival and is one of the world's richest cities per capita.[8]

Creative communities can promote competitiveness. Knowledge innovation, and the development and marketing of trademarks and brands can result from such communities. Theme-oriented or creative product communities are sources of innovation in their own fields. In addition, ideas and concepts penetrate into other socio-economic fields.

[8] Chen Junxia, 'Film Festival becomes the Economic Engine,' *Market News China*, 2005 (12).

Creative communities produce both implicit and explicit effects. Implicit effects refer to platforms and activities that produce regular or irregular exchange of ideas on related themes. The outcomes are intangible resources that may produce new value or become industry benchmarks. The impact of the World Economic Forum (WEF) is an example of implicit effects. A non-profit organization, WEF is a platform for business leaders, politicians and academics to discuss collaborative approaches to global issues. Held annually in Davos, Switzerland since 1971, the forum is known as the 'Economic United Nations'. It is in fact a typical 'creative community' featuring clear themes and equal exchange of ideas. More than 2,400 political and business leaders from all over the world gather here every year to discuss topics of world concern, such as the oil crisis, global warming and financial risks. The theme of 2008 was 'the power of collaboration and innovation'.

At WEF, everybody is a participant. No assistant is allowed into the venue. Whether you are a CEO of a big company, billionaire or a pop star, you have to carry your own luggage, do your own check-in and line up for cloakroom service. You fill your own water cup and get your own conference materials. At the pre-dinner cocktail party prime ministers, like everybody else, elbow their way in the crowds. There is no designated seating in the theatre and whoever comes late has to stand in the aisles. There is equal opportunity for everyone too when it comes to discussions and debates. Equal participation and exchange is practiced by involving the public in the discussion of major issues. On the WEF official website, people can submit video responses to set questions and WEF participants will watch the highest rated video and engage with them. An exchange and interaction between WEF and the wider public is thus formed. WEF's positive impact on world development is for everyone to see. Mandela once commented in public, 'without WEF, South Africa's fate would have been totally different.' Former United Nations Secretary General Kofi Annan believes 'WEF has satisfied people's need for a new world.' Klaus Martin Schwab, Founder of WEF, holds multiple positions and functions,[9] but he identifies himself as 'an artist or a creator,' being the renowned leader of the WEF creative community.

---

[9] Klaus Martin Schwab, Founder and Executive Chairman of the World Economic Forum, Co-founder (1998) of the Schwab Foundation for Social Entrepreneurship, founder (2004) of The Forum of Young Global Leaders. The knighthood (KCMG) was bestowed by H.M. the Queen of England.

The impact of WEF is a result of a direct link to innovative outcomes; the symbolic value of culture and the arts is effectively transformed into social and market benefits.

The 'Impression Series,' a series of stage performances featuring local landscapes has produced a brand effect with tangible economic benefits. Produced by an innovative team led by the film director Zhang Yimou, the Impression brand has been exported to other countries. The symbolic value of culture has greatly increased the competitiveness of local industries and brought new dynamics for social and economic development. 'Impression · Sanjie Liu' was first performed in 2004 in Yangshuo County in the south-western city of Guilin. Since then the commercial and cultural value of the scenic spot where the show was staged has increased and land values of neighbouring areas have increased five-fold. The show has boosted the local economy of Yangshuo County by a similar ratio with tourism incomes increasing by 100 million RMB per year.

Creative communities facilitate cross-industry integration. The huge impact of creative industries comes from the formation of the industrial chain and the reinvestment of creative outputs. The key is marketing.

Creative outputs have often become investment factors for other industries as well as providing new value elements for consumers. Mickey Mouse, Barbie dolls, Harry Potter, Mashimaro and Hello Kitty are all the result of creative outputs. Once a brand is established, it penetrates into other industries including toys, stationery, clothes and accessories, luggage and food. As a result, the value added of these industries increases. Music can be encoded into chips and integrated into products to increase their value. Creative design and planning can help almost all traditional industries open up the 'Blue Ocean' and promote the development of related industries. What is more important, however, is that literacy is improved and creativity is encouraged.

Business and consumer communities are the two major drivers of cross-industry convergence. Creative outputs have specialized marketing and consumption services. For example, independent agents, professional brokers and exhibition organizers are typical profit-oriented operators. They utilize personal and social networks to integrate ideas, capital, product and markets for the formation of the creative industrial chain. There are also non-profit promoting communities, such as creative industries associations, network alliances of creative cities and marketing organizations for public culture and art.

They serve as third parties in promoting the integration of creative industries with related industries and facilitating in other non-creative industries.

The Creative Society

Richard Florida's *The Flight of the Creative Class* focuses on one of the hottest economic topics today: the global war for creative talent and the importance of building more creative societies. Florida says this is important 'because wherever talent goes, innovation, creativity, and economic growth are sure to follow.' He adds 'Today, the terms of competition revolve around a central axis: a nation's ability to mobilize, attract, and retain human creative talent.'[10]

In 2007, John Hartley proposed that creative industries are developing toward a kind of 'creative society.' He described the evolution of creative industries from creative clusters (output) to creative service (input) and further to the creative citizen (consumer) or the creative society.[11]

Desmond Hui, director of the Centre for Culture and Development, Chinese University of Hong Kong, believes that discussions of creative industries at policy level, such as wealth and employment creation are a necessary basis and premise for developing creative industries. However, he points out, this is not the whole content or the fundamental goal of creative industries. The transformation and restructuring of society is the highest achievement of creative industries which aim to develop every individual's potential creativity in addition to developing the economy and society.[12]

Creative industries need a 'social structure of creativity.' Studies of the creative society across the world have broken through regional boundaries and cultural differences. They have come to the consensus of 'accepting differences and seeking common ground.' The 'differences' relate to development approach, industry focus and policy support due to various forms of economic

---

[10] Richard Florida 'America's Looming Creativity Crisis,' *Harvard Business Review*. Oct 2005. Available: http://hbr.org/2004/10/americas-looming-creativity-crisis/ar/1 [accessed 8 March 2011].

[11] John Hartley 'The evolution of the creative industries – Creative clusters, creative citizens and social network markets,' Presentation Creative Industries Conference, Asia-Pacific Week, Sept 2007, Berlin.

[12] Desmond Hui. 'Creative Industries are not only Economic Issues,' an interview by *Cultural Industry Weekly*, Vol. 5, 2006, pp. 21. Available: http://www.ccdy.cn/2005-07/22/content_236821.htm [accessed 8 March 2011].

foundation, human environment, policy systems and talent structure. The 'common ground' here is about being innovation-led and making a sustainable creative society the ultimate goal.

I have been interviewed by the media many times. Whenever a reporter asks me what kind of social environment is needed, I stress the importance of three soft elements, openness, tolerance and diversity. Whether it is China's ancient civilization and wisdom or Western individual expression and innovative spirit, a tolerant atmosphere is needed for the development of creative industries. Cultural tolerance allows creative industries to grow. Innovation and creativity are always associated with passion. It is hard to imagine how great ideas could ever develop in a conservative social atmosphere. When we talk about creating a social atmosphere in which creativity is respected, we are not simply talking about paying attention to those people already established in their respective fields. We should also pay due attention to those creative professionals by providing them with moral and financial support. This is very important in terms of inspiring creativity, attracting creative people and constructing a creative social ecology.

Although there is no specific discourse relating to 'creative industries' in the United States, the creative economy there is highly developed with regular cutting-edge scientific innovations and a diversity of products and art forms. US media and entertainment products, in particular, are popular across the world. The competitiveness of America's creative economy is supported by a powerful social structure of creativity, or what we call 'the creative social ecology.' This kind of social ecology is the soft environment key to the development of creative industries and the creative economy. In the ecological system of creative industries, creative communities are the most active basic units which maintain the dynamics of this ecology. Creative communities at various levels constitute the 'social ecology chain' from where creativity takes roots and grows.

Under the forces of globalization, business tends to gather in areas where creative people are clustered. Conventional thinking holds that economic development is made possible by enterprises because it is the enterprise that attracts skilled people. But today's practice turns that idea on its head: it is availability of skilled people that increasingly attracts business and capital. This has overthrown the conventional wisdom that 'industries tend to move toward low-cost regions.' A city's competitiveness now depends on whether the city has a solid social structure of creativity and a supporting infrastructure, posing new challenges for city policy makers. Policy makers should try to ascertain what young people are looking for. Many young people are looking for jobs that will allow them some autonomy and the ability to express their creativity. They do not want to work passively. When an individual's creativity is fully released and applied to industry, it is the individual who is driving the company, and even the regional economy, forward. Encouraging creativity and acknowledging the value of creativity will give rise to investment, production and consumption of creative industries.

This phenomenon of industries attracted to where creative talents concentrate can be explained by Richard Florida's study of 'the social structure of creativity,' which consists of three parts: a new system appropriate for scientific innovation and creative institutions (such as a financial system interested in investing in creative industries, high-tech development companies, and sustainable research funding), a more effective innovative model of products and services (such as a work environment where employees can release their creativity, a flexible production approach and a convenient exchange and exhibition platform) and a social and cultural environment for creative production (such as a lifestyle attractive to creative talents, a tolerant social atmosphere and a cultural system that encourages avant-garde art expressions).[13]

The social ecology suitable for creative industries can be measured by the creativity index constructed by Florida. The creativity index consists of four parts: 1) the creative class share of the workforce, 2) the innovation index measured as patents per capita, 3) the high-tech index consisting of two factors: (a) the output of an area's high-tech industries expressed as a percentage of the output of the nation's high-tech industries, and (b) a ratio of the level of an area's output from high-tech industries to the level of the nation's output from high-tech industries; and 4) the degree of diversity measured by the Gay Index, the Bohemian Index, the Talent index and the Melting Pot index.

A good and appropriate creative social ecology is not only the basic condition for creative industries but also the necessary foundation for the rise of creative communities. For cities and regions intent on a creative economy, the key is to build a good social ecology appropriate for the growth of creative

---

[13] Richard Florida, *The Rise of the Creative Class and How It's Transforming Work, Leisure, Community and Everyday Life*. (New York: Basic Books, 2002).

communities. This social ecology should include a comfortable work and life environment and a tolerant cultural atmosphere in which creative talents can work happily and give full and free rein to their creativity.

Tolerance

Creative industries, in particular, need tolerance. As the foundation of creativity, cultural diversity requires a tolerant environment. A tolerant social environment and a relaxed cultural atmosphere will help further liberate creative professionals to think outside the box and to stimulate their creativity, allowing personality, talent and the interests of each individual to be respected and developed. To a large extent, so-called creativity consists of a change in the traditional mode of thinking, perhaps even the subversion of a traditional sense of reality. It champions the continuous production of the new to replace the old. Innovation requires an all-out transformation ranging from the individual to the society. It promotes social progress by continuously challenging existing technologies and models. Tolerance means keeping an open mind to new things. In other words, it means the willingness to trust and tolerate in cases where the new can seem hard to accept for the time being. A tolerant environment, including a general openness in society, the tolerance of different opinions, the encouragement of innovation, equal opportunity and life chances, will enable people to work and live happily and enjoy their achievements.

Free expression is a very important index of tolerance. The freedom I am talking about here is not in the moral or ethical sense but in the sense of thinking freely, experimenting freely and conducting business freely. It is the freedom to express and pursue ideas and to have the opportunity to test those ideas to see if they work. The internet is becoming increasingly important in people's life as it can provide the maximum freedom for people to post their opinions and ideas on the net without having to ask for anyone's permission. The free use of the internet has brought wonderful changes to our lives and has made 'everything possible', as the words from the Olympic Gymnast Li Ning's branding remind us.

Tolerance is like a 'pass' to the creative social ecology, allowing various 'new things' to survive, grow and face challenges. My old friend John Howkins used to describe creative industries as 'frustrated industries' due to the fact that there are many failures in the creative economy. All the explorations of the unknown world, whether in terms of cultural creativity or of technological innovation, are a kind of test of new methods or new models which carry a high degree of uncertainty. So it is no surprise that there is a high rate of failure. Only ideas that have undergone numerous tests produce dynamic effects and positively impact the development of creative industries, the formation of the creative economy and even the construction of the creative society. Tolerance can hardly be accomplished overnight. Many new things are rejected in the beginning, which can be exemplified by the case of the Twelve Girls Band[14] and the *Kung Fu Panda* movie. People started to accept them after an initial rejection. If we do not allow this and do not allow that, how could we expect to develop creative industries? Creative industries in China took off late compared with some other countries and regions and it takes time to go through the process of change from the old way of thinking to the practice of innovation. The controversies, doubts and restrictions that plague the initial development stage of creative industries are all understandable. We should be tolerant even of 'intolerant' behaviours. Apart from tolerance, of course, we should be confident and patient in allowing time to test these new developments.

Tolerance is also a lubricant for the smooth running of 'the creative machine,' capable not only of penetrating into and coordinating every link of the creative industries but also of penetrating into and coordinating the social spaces in which we live and work. As we know, creative industries involve both the production sector and the circulation and distribution sectors. Tolerance in turn should involve the media and the audience. An enabling media environment and a tolerant public do no harm in inspiring individual creativity and releasing cultural productivity. Moreover, in today's internet age, the user can participate in the process of innovation. So tolerance is needed for the growth of education, media and the internet, all of which are closely related to creative industries. I believe, rather than rushing to negative conclusions, we should tolerate anything new as long as it is not harmful

[14] An introduction to Twelve Girls Band is available at http://www.ccdy.cn/2005-07/22/content_236821.htm [accessed 8 March 2011].

to society. We should change our old ways of thinking to change with the times. We should do the same with cultural heritage. When developing our historical and cultural resources, we need to bear in mind that we should carry on tradition but not be bound by it. We should introduce modern elements in an appropriate way. Only by doing so can we expect to stimulate consumption and to play an active role in promoting the creative economy and the creative society.

Regions with a developed creative economy are often those where creative people and high-tech industries are clustering together and where tolerance is most expressed. In general, the creative class tends to choose to live and work in places with more tolerance and diversity. The creative class does not allow work to dominate everything. Members of the creative class would rather choose a place to live first and then start looking for a job. A city's economic prosperity is no longer determined by favourable tax policies or cheap natural resources such as electricity and land. The core of the creative economy is the 'creative workforce.' Social environments that champion openness, tolerance and cultural diversity and attract the creative class to work and live there achieve economic success. This kind of environment and atmosphere are often closely related to the cultural characteristics and openness of a city. As China's economic centre and future international finance centre, Shanghai is known for its open-mindedness, a place where eastern and western lifestyles meet. But these are only the external expressions of Shanghai culture. The internal essence of the Shanghai culture is tolerance and the pursuit of novelty. Both internal and external factors constitute an enabling social environment for the free flow of creative people and for Shanghai's progress towards the status of creative capital.

Social Capital

Social capital is the basis for creative industries and the creative economy to progress toward the creative society. The rise of various creative communities has helped form the creative society which includes not only the creative class (communities of creative people) and creative clusters (communities of creative enterprises) but also the consumers of creative products, various non-profit organizations and corresponding educational institutions for creative talents.

All these communities are of long-term significance for promoting creative industries, the creative economy and the creative society.

Consumer capital

In the age of the creative economy, consumers have become a form of production capital and an organic link in the creative industrial chain, in the general process of a creative product from R&D, into production and to marketing and sales. Consumer capital is invested in the two ends of the chain and forms the feedback mechanism of the creative industrial chain. In addition to organizing production and sales according to consumer demand, creative industries also develop the consumer resources into industrial capital and a new source for the realization of value.

Consumer capital promotes creative industries in two ways. One is for consumers to become a leading power for innovation. Almost every person in the society is a consumer and thus can add value to a creative product, especially when digital and interactive technologies have enabled non-professionals and ordinary consumers to directly participate in innovative and creative activities. Innovation from consumers can enter future commercial development and production via certain forms of R&D. The Open Source movement, individual customization in industrial design, computer games and even the endings of TV drama serials are typical examples. Another is via consumer investment in the expression and pursuit of individual cultural, social and creative values. This kind of investment will eventually become value added for creative industries or the creative economy. Behind the popularity of 'Reality TV' shows are the personalized choices and self-identification of various kinds of consumers. Multimedia channels such as SMS and the internet have provided popular and cheap channels for this kind of personalized communication. Similarly, fan groups appear to be chasing stars, but in essence this kind of activity is the external expression of the audience's identification with their own values and an investment in values with which they identify. These fans may appear crazy sometimes and may be difficult to comprehend in terms of the law of economic benefits but as a matter of fact, their activities have greatly promoted the development of the creative industries.

Obviously, creative industries rely heavily on the expanding scale of personal choice. Their survival is increasingly determined by user participation.

In other words, the investment of consumer capital determines how well creative industries will develop.

Education capital

Education capital is the cornerstone of the creative industry. Creative people cannot be trained overnight. Investment in future creative talent requires a strong educational infrastructure, a new creative education mechanism and new policies that encourage lifelong education. These will be the drivers of education capital to promote creative industries and the creative economy as well as being the foundation of the creative society.

The education system for the creative society cannot do without a sound educational infrastructure which should be able to fulfil some key functions such as the cultivation of a base for new types of creative talent, providing a training place for newly-recruited creative workers, an experimental space for new art forms and products and a performing venue for old or new artists from various fields.

Re-modelling the education mechanism may well be the most challenging breakthrough yet for China's education system today. However, it will be the most fundamental and effective initiative for the cultivation of creative talent. The construction of a new education system requires a multi-channel and multi-form education mechanism that includes the provision of creative education opportunities for everyone, developing individual creative potential and providing more practical activities for working with artists. A creative education mechanism should break through the bondage of the traditional education system and establish a new teaching concept and a new curriculum. The disciplinary barriers, in particular, should be opened up so as to cultivate 'generalists.' It requires the coordinated efforts of various parties to cultivate creative talents. Therefore a diversified approach involving interaction between schools, industries and communities should be established. Emphasis should be put on innovative humanistic education so that young people's 'creative impulse' and 'enjoyment of creativity' is inspired and cultivated. This would radically change the current exam-oriented practice that stifles innovative thinking. Currently, Beijing University of Aeronautics & Astronautics, Peking University and the Communication University of China are experimenting with the cultivation of talent for cultural and creative industries by establishing new courses and related majors. With the progress of cultural and creative industries, more cultivation models such as the alliance of campus-based enterprises and integrated education of university-industry research will need to be experimented with beyond tertiary education. Some social institutions engaged in vocational education are carrying out similar experiments.

The key to accumulating creative education capital is to make policies that can provide lifelong education for creative people. Effective civil education throughout various social organizations will generate productivity for the creative economy and consumers for creative products. This means that production and the producer, as well as consumption and the consumer, are creation-oriented, as a result of which the quality of life of the nation will be effectively improved. A large number of top-level, highly specialized education and training institutions are behind New York City's status as the world's creative centre. Global art elite institution The Juilliard School provides the best professional training in the world for dancers, musicians and actors. Visual art professionals can seek help from New York University's Tisch College of Liberal Arts, the Visual Arts College and the PAT Institute that are among America's best academies of fine arts. If you are an aspiring dancer, the American Ballet Academy will be the best choice. Fashion designers can choose the famous New York Fashion Institute of Technology and Parsons School of Design while architects may choose the Construction Union, New York City Art Association or the Centre for Architecture in New York City, all of which are top-level education institutions.

Non-profit organization capital

Non-profit organizations (NPOs) are one of the key elements of the creative infrastructure. The unique organizational and operational mechanism of NPOs contributes to the high enthusiasm of participants who are a group of people gathered together for a common goal. These participants are business partners in pursuit of realizing their own values instead of economic gains. This 'volunteer-style' of self-consciousness and persistence is hard to find in economic organizations in general and makes it easier for NPOs to achieve their goals. By utilizing their social powers for problem-solving, social groups or communities with various functions become the driving force for transforming 'economic society' to 'creative society'. The goals of NPOs are not the maximization of profits but the realization of their vision – the maximization of social benefits. By consciously devoting themselves to the vision, non-profit organizations are creating social wealth and accumulating social capital.

In Shanghai non-profit organizations have played a big role in the rapid development of creative industries in recent years. These organizations mainly include the Shanghai Creative Industries Association (SCIA), the Shanghai Creative Industries Centre (SCIC) and the Research Centre for Creative Industries, Shanghai Academy of Social Sciences (RCCI SASS). SCIA assists the municipal government and industry in the integration of resources, the coordination of various parties and the exchange of information. SCIC is focused on practical operations, cluster planning and investment assistance while the RCCI SASS studies experiences, shares knowledge and theories as well as promoting education. The three parties have jointly organized a number of major activities, such as the Shanghai International Forum of Creative Industries, the Shanghai International Week of Creative Industries and the Creative Design Competition. These non-profit organizations related to creative industries have not only contributed to the rapid development of creative industries in Shanghai and the formation of creative communities but have also provided consultation, planning, lecture and training services for other cities in China. They have strengthened their exchange with domestic and international creative institutions and attracted a large number of creative talents.

Gross National Happiness (GNH)

When economic development reaches a certain stage, people's understanding of development will change accordingly. In Japan, GNC (Gross National Cool) is becoming a key index for Japan's economy. The most active enterprises in the Japanese economy are now those SMEs focused on developing business based on personal experiences. Their products are outside the range of traditional growth index but are in effect improving Japanese people's welfare.

In our persistent pursuit of GDP, have we neglected the real purpose of increasing national wealth? A wealthy nation does not necessarily mean a happy nation. Lester Brown, director of the Earth Policy Institute of the United States, cautioned China in 2005 that China should readjust its GDP-centred development model and take the approach of people-oriented sustainable development in pursuit of its people's happiness. In the same way that GDP and GNP are used to measure a country's and a nation's wealth, we should also use GNH (Gross National Happiness) to measure people's happiness.

GDP is an index to measure a country's wealth. But it can neither reflect the quality of economic growth and the cost involved, nor measure the level of social welfare and the degree of people's happiness. In many cases, GDP growth may obscure a decrease of people's welfare as health and happiness are difficult to present in the form of statistics. GNH, on the other hand, is the barometer of social conditions and people's life, measuring people's living standards and reflecting the degree of people's satisfaction with life and their sense of happiness.

One significant result of China's thirty years of reform and opening up is the continuous double-digit growth of its economy. Even during the 2008–2009 global financial crisis China maintained over 8 per cent growth in GDP. China has become the third largest economy in the world. The country is becoming stronger and the people are becoming better off. But has our sense of happiness increased accordingly? According to the three surveys on the happiness index of the Chinese people in a recent ten-year period, conducted by Professor Ruut Veenhoven of Erasmus University in the Netherlands, the national happiness index for 1990 was 6.64 (on a scale of 1–10), up to 7.08 in 1995 and down to 6.60 in 2001. This shows that even continuous, rapid economic growth cannot guarantee a continuous growth in people's happiness. Happiness and wealth do not always grow synchronously. When wealth is accumulated to a certain degree, its marginal effect on happiness is decreased.

China needs GDP to develop its economy. GNH, however, is more important in increasing the quality of life and general happiness of its people. Creative industries can make unique contributions to the latter. As mentioned earlier, apart from generating wealth and employment, creative industries' biggest contribution will be the transformation of the whole society. Creative industries promote human development while developing the economy. In China today where a series of problems, such as property prices, healthcare welfare, education, food safety, environmental pollution and the urban–rural gap, are raising doubts about, and challenging, the one-dimensional pursuit of economic growth, we need to pay more attention to people's livelihood, humanity and ecology. This requires us to improve social welfare and increase people's sense of happiness while developing the economy. The transformation of our approach to economic development and the promotion of coordinated social development should be our agenda.

Lifestyle

Many foreigners in Shanghai like to go to Xintiandi for a cup of coffee, a chat with friends or a movie, or just to have a walk along the stone-paved walkways to relax and to get a feel of the Shanghai-style living. Xintiandi used to be a neighbourhood of old tenements of a kind found only in Shanghai. It has been turned into a stylish, car-free district of clubs, restaurants and boutiques by a process of restoration considered to be China's finest historical redevelopment project. It is more than just a tourist destination. It has become the epitome of the modern urbanites' lifestyle. To have a party or have a cup of coffee there is now a way of spending leisure for culturally-savvy local residents as well as foreign visitors.

Creativity is the leading edge of these new lifestyles as creative consumer goods attract people's attention. Culture adds new symbolic value to products and reconstructs people's attitude toward life. In contemporary society, popular culture champions fashion and trends, thus giving prominent display to novelty, the short time span and the strong audio and video effects of cultural products. All the fields included in creative industries, such as advertising, architecture, art & antique, arts & craft, design, fashion design, the movie industry, interactive leisure software, music, performing art, publishing, software, broadcasting, games and net games, animation, DV, Flash, SMS, mobile value-added services and network video, rely heavily on new ideas and new designs. The various experiential products, a kind of integration of entertainment culture, leisure culture and fashion culture, are advocating a fashionable trend of 'bringing art to life and life to art' through interactive experiences and pleasurable consumption. These products are creating a new lifestyle and have improved people's quality of life.

John Ellis, Dean of the Department of Media Arts at Royal Holloway, University of London, believes creative industries can define people's choice of lifestyle by providing opportunities for people to produce their own images. They can enable people to express their own identities and personalities while giving them inspiration.

Creative clusters are the physical carriers of the creative industries. Their unique form of industry clustering and spatial layout has given rise to new lifestyles, such as loft living and the bohemian settlements of SOHO. The new lifestyle of combining work, life and entertainment has, in terms of time and space, broken the traditional division of office workspace, living quarters and entertainment areas. Since the 1990s, loft living has gradually become the most personalized, avant-garde and fashionable lifestyle. Artists and designers divided abandoned industrial plants into different spaces for living, work, social networking, entertainment and storage and created new lifestyles and new art trends. In China, we have various kinds of creative spaces, such as the 798 Space in Beijing, the Kunming Loft in Kunming, Tianzifang and M50 in Shanghai and LOFT 49 in Hangzhou. These creative spaces have provided a very different work and lifestyle for creative workers than those working in the industrial era.

The West End in London and Broadway in New York are world-famous centres of performing arts. Going to a musical in the West End has become the thing to do, with three quarters of foreign tourists putting this on their itinerary. In Shanghai, it has become a fashionable lifestyle choice and even a habit for young people to go to the theatre on Anfu Road. Only ten years ago, only the elderly were theatre-goers in Shanghai (The same happened on Broadway). Today, the Shanghai Dramatic Arts Centre on Anfu Road is filled with 'dark-haired' audiences, 80 per cent of whom are young people under forty. From the perspective of the creative industries, performing art, as a core content of creative industries, has produced an experiential product – drama which is driving the trend for 'bringing life to art and art to life' for the audience through the exploitation of on-the-spot experience and consumer sentiment. As a symbol of cultural consumption, Anfu Road is not only staging popular theatre performances but also generating a creative atmosphere by injecting imaginative elements of fashion into the city.

Quality of Life

'Life' is a word with rich and profound meaning. Fundamentally, life consists of the human activities of survival and development along with vitality and creativity. 'Quality of life' refers to five components of everyday life, namely economic life, cultural life, political life, social life, and environmental life. According to Rostow's theory[15] in his book *The Stages of Economic Growth*, the highest stage of regional economic development is characterized by the pursuit of quality of life as the final marker. Creative industries can improve people's quality of life in economic, cultural, environmental and social terms.[16]

Some fields of the creative industries, industrial design, for example, can greatly upgrade the level and standard of existing manufacturing industries. This will contribute to the improvement of the quality of people's economic life.

Most products of creative industries are cultural products which will help satisfy people's diverse cultural needs and thus will help improve the quality of people's cultural life.

Creative industries exhaust almost none of the non-renewable material resources. Some fields, in particular architectural design and landscape design, are closely related to urban upgrading which will contribute to the improvement of the quality of people's environmental life.

Cultural and leisure tourism and the cultural exhibition sector of the creative industries will certainly help improve the quality of people's social life.

To build a 'city of high life quality' has become an intrinsic motivation for creative industries in Hangzhou, a city known as 'capital of leisure' and 'Silicon Valley in Paradise.' In addition to creating wealth and employment, creative industries can integrate life with business and the environment in a perfect combination, thus contributing to Hangzhou's effort to improve its people's quality of life. The lifestyle of combining leisure, culture and business, or in other words the combination of tourism & leisure, cultural creativity and the local elements of tea culture and traditional Chinese medicine, is most attractive to the creative class as this combination integrates business with life as well as culture with economy. Unlike some other metropolises such as Beijing, Shanghai and Shenzhen, Hangzhou has its unique natural environment and cultural atmosphere. People's attitude to life, their living conditions and lifestyles in Hangzhou can be compared with those of many European countries.

[15] Walt Whitman Rostow, *The Stages of Economic Growth* (Cambridge: Cambridge University Press, 1960, 1971, 1990).
[16] Bingbing Wang, *Thoughts about Stimulating the Development of Cultural and Creative Industries*. http://www.zj.xinhuanet.com/website/2008-10/10/content_14605164.htm [accessed 8 March 2011].

Employment

It is estimated that by 2020, the global core creative industries will achieve a business turnover of US$8,000 billion.[17] China's development orientation is attracting world attention. How can China transform from a manufacturing country with cost as its key competitive card to a creative economy with innovation as the main competitive advantage? One important factor will be the cultivation and employment direction of creative talent. Between 2000 and 2015, there will be 85 million Chinese young people graduating from universities.[18] Whether these graduates want to take creative jobs will affect the employment direction of creative talent in the future. It's fair to say that creative industries are not only creating new employment opportunities for Chinese society but also changing the traditional employment structure of China.

Globally, creative industries took off in the midst of readjustment of the urban economic structure. The concept of creative industries is the result of the old industrial cities' effort to deal with the problems of high energy consumption, high pollution and low value added brought about by backward manufacturing industries. In the transformation of the urban economy, creative industries have obtained good capital and conditions in which they have been able to create more employment opportunities. Taking advantage of a talent pool created by clustering, a smooth flow of information, sound infrastructure and closeness to the market that cities can provide, creative industries have become the development orientation of cities. On the one hand, the broad fields covered by creative industries can accommodate a large population of labour while the 'spillover effect' brought about by creative industries and the integration of emerging industries will give birth to more creative enterprises as new carriers of smart employment. On the other hand, some emerging creative enterprises will provide new employment for a large number of well-educated professionals and college graduates. This will help construct a harmonious society where people can work and live happily.

---

[17] According to John Howkins estimation in his report 'The Global Creative Economy 2000–2015,' available: http://www.icecngo.org/tourga/abc17.html [accessed 8 March 2011].
[18] See John Howkins' foreword to this book.

In Shanghai, the flourishing creative industries have provided opportunities for university graduates to start up their own business. To cater to people's pursuit of personality and fashion, an increasing number of new professions and trades have been established. According to the city's labour market report for the third quarter of 2007 (the peak employment period of university graduates), there were 1,200 creative positions available covering graphic design, jewellery design and production, landscape design, digital video software design and production, furniture and home furnishing, toys, home textiles, flowers and ceramics. A report on Shanghai's digital content industry shows that the industry employed 139,400 people in 2006, 2.9 times the figure from 2002.[19]

Employment provided by creative industries is different from traditional employment which has varying requirements for individual applicants. Because creative industries are borderless, creative people are not evaluated by their professional background and educational qualifications. Their creativity is evaluated by their ability to accomplish a project. Service industries in the United States and Britain have accounted for two thirds of each country's GDP while manufacturing industries have lost their appeal to young people who are more interested in working with their creative imagination. In contrast to the comparatively saturated manufacturing enterprises, creative industries in China have great employment potential.

The strategic changes brought about by creative industries, such as the industrial restructuring, the upgrade of production capacity and the transformation of urban functions, have improved employment structure as well as economic structure. Employment is transforming from being labour-intensive to knowledge-intensive. Employment in creative industries will see a significant increase. In the USA, 40 per cent of jobs are related to creativity in the sense that these jobs require workers to be creative, to challenge traditional practices and to come up with new approaches. Creative industries in America and Britain, in particular, grew by 14 per cent and 12 per cent respectively.[20]

In addition to changing employment structures, creative industries have new solutions to forms of employment. While the traditional labour contract

[19] Shanghai Digital Content Industry Whitebook 2008–2009, research report by Shanghai Digital Content Industry Promotion Centre, Aug 2009. www.chinadcic.org.cn [accessed 8 March 2011].
[20] John Howkins, *The Creative Economy: How People Make Money from Ideas* (London: Penguin, 2001).

provides fixed-term, static employment, employment in creative industries tends to be dynamic, flexible and short-term. Formal employment is changing into informal employment with outsourcing and freelance working becoming increasingly popular. The existence of large numbers of creative enterprises has provided a network-type space for the survival of informal employment. In London, many jobs in the creative art fields, such as music, TV, film and media, are project-based and short-term. Creative professionals are bound to a project and could be working in the same company or a different company depending on where the project is. For example, the animation industry in Britain has created at least 5,000 jobs and the computer games industry around 9,000. But more jobs, classified as 'hidden employment,' are not included in the statistics. These jobs, including between 37 and 57 per cent of animation workers, are in the form of freelance work in some very small companies. Thanks to the internet which provides new forms of work, life and entertainment and makes mobile working possible, the creative class have the opportunity to break the bondage of a labour contract. They advocate working freelance, a flexible working style and a changing workplace. They prefer serving a broader field with their creative input. For the members of the SOHO community, employment needs to be redefined.

These new developments in employment are making it increasingly necessary to carry out a comprehensive reform of culture, education, urban development, the market, intellectual property and internationalization policies. The cultivation of creative talent, has become the most urgent task for China in developing its creative industries. Talent is crucial to the development of creative industries and lack of talent has now become the 'bottleneck' in the development process. The one huge challenge for the future development of China will be how to cultivate talent that can cater to the specific needs of creative industries. Right now, I would like to look at Britain, the cradle of creative industries, and see how they are going about it.

Creative industries are the second largest high-growth industries in terms of employment in London, with one in every five new jobs coming from creative industries. Creative industries have become one of London's biggest industry sectors with output and employment second only to business services. Statistics indicate that by 2012 when the Olympic Games is held in London, the output value of London's creative industries will be 30 billion pounds, outpacing the financial sector to become the top-performing industry. The Greater London

Authority, recognizing the employment potential of creative industries, has begun to provide training, infrastructure and new channels of investment for creative projects. London Urban Collective is one of the organizations that provide training for young people who need diversified skills to enter the music industry. The series of government policies and social initiatives for creative industries have helped London maintain and enhance its reputation as 'the world's creative and cultural centre.' The creative industry sector in Britain is the largest in scale anywhere in the world. The creative industries have become key national assets for Britain.

To sum up, we should make good use of any means, whether economic hard power or cultural 'soft power' to promote creative industries toward human-oriented development, economic prosperity and sustainable social development, as long as these forces can be effectively transformed into a comprehensive strength that will stimulate creative industries and the creative economy to develop into the creative society.

Index